D1400087

FORWARD MISSION STUDY COURSES

EDITED UNDER THE DIRECTION OF THE

MISSIONARY EDUCATION MOVEMENT
OF THE UNITED STATES AND CANADA

THE CHURCH OF THE OPEN COUNTRY

N. B.—Special helps and denominational mission study literature for this course can be obtained by corresponding with the Secretary of your mission board or society.

WARREN H. WILSON

THE CHURCH
OF THE
OPEN COUNTRY

*A Study of the Church for the
Working Farmer*

BY

WARREN H. WILSON, *1867-*

AUTHOR OF "QUAKER HILL"

NEW YORK

Missionary Education Movement of the
United States and Canada

1911

TO MY WIFE

WITH WHOM EVERY MEMORY OF THE COUNTRY
IS ASSOCIATED

THE COUNTRY CHURCH

BY L. H. BAILEY

I stand in the fields,
Where the wide earth yields
  Her bounties of fruit and grain;
Where the furrows turn
Till the plowshares burn
  As they come 'round and 'round again;
Where the workers pray
With their tools all day
  In sunshine and shadow and rain.

And I bid them tell
Of the crops they sell
  And speak of the work they have done;
I speed every man
In his hope and plan
  And follow his day with the sun;
And grasses and trees,
The birds and the bees
  I know and I feel ev'ry one.

And out of it all
As the seasons fall
  I build my great temple alway;
I point to the skies,
But my footstone lies
  In commonplace work of the day;
For I preach the worth
Of the native earth—
  To love and to work is to pray.

CONTENTS

ILLUSTRATIONS

PREFACE

THERE are not a few who ask the question, "What is the use of the Church in the open country?" Some of them have through a defective training learned to value their own souls dear and the Church very cheaply. Having secured a sort of fire insurance against the next world, they care nothing for an efficient Church in this world. But the religious history of the country community demonstrates that an efficient Church is necessary to the salvation of souls. Others there are who hold, as a matter of theory, that all rural institutions should be assembled at the population centers, presumably at the railway stations, and that ultimately the farmers will follow their stores, schools, and churches, and will live in congested villages; going out mornings to their fields, and returning in the evening to sleep. But the course of American history indicates no such future peopling of the land. It becomes the Church to serve the farmer where he lives.

An increasing number of American farmers are under economic pressure. They cannot secure land, and they have little ownership in productive tools. They, too, ask the question as to the utility of the Church in the country. They feel that they cannot afford anything but necessities. It is the purpose of these chapters to describe the Church which is a necessity to the poor. In the open country four farmers out of ten are renters. The future of the Church is with them. Yet they are to-day included in the membership of the churches in the smallest proportions of all men in the country. To give them the gospel is the acute problem of the Church in the open country.

I am indebted, for help in the preparing of this book, above all to Miss Anna B. Taft, without whose help it would have been impossible; and to my loyal associates in the day's work, every one of whom has given an essential part to a task completed in the midst of travel and teaching.

Warren H. Wilson.

New York, *October* 25, 1911.

RURAL DECAY AND REPAIR

The well-read town dweller has more to learn about the social problems of the farm than the well-read farmer has to learn about the problems of the town. Each, however, ought to know the other's problems, for the problems of each are the problems of the other. They are all problems of the nation. As long as all men, however, derive their living from the soil, so long will the problems of the farmer be the fundamental problems of the nation. Until recently on account of the great development in industrial conditions, the problems of the town and the city have seemed most insistent; but now the more fundamental problems—the problems of the agriculturist—are making themselves heard.—*The Outlook*

We conclude, then, that the farm problem consists in maintaining upon our farms a class of people who have succeeded in procuring for themselves the highest possible class status, not only in the industrial, but in the political and the social order—a relative status, moreover, that is measured by the demands of American ideals. The farm problem thus connects itself with the whole question of democratic civilization. This is not mere platitude. For we cannot properly judge the significance and the relation of the different industrial activities of our farmers, and especially the value of the various social agencies for rural betterment, except by the standard of class status. It is here that we seem to find the only satisfactory philosophy of rural progress.—*K. L. Butterfield*

The patriotic American, who thinks of the life of the nation rather than of the individual, will, if he looks beneath the surface, discern in this God-prospered country symptoms of rural decadence fraught with danger to national efficiency.—*Horace Plunkett*

In the United States it should be remembered that nowadays peace strength is quite as important as war strength, and it may be questioned whether there can be any sustained industrial efficiency where the great body of workers who conduct the chief—the only absolutely necessary—industry are wasting the resources at their command by bad husbandry.—*Horace Plunkett*

I

RURAL DECAY AND REPAIR

Widespread Untoward Conditions. It is the common opinion of rural leaders that country life in America has fallen out of repair. The household, the church, the school, and the store in the country show the effect of change. They are not what they were twenty-five years ago. These changes are seen all over the United States, with slight local variation. They are uniform from Maine to Mississippi. Young people are leaving the country for the city, teachers of country schools move almost every year, and many ministers have despaired of the country Church.

National Commission. The Country Life Commission, in their report to President Theodore Roosevelt, in 1908, made this a national issue. Writers before that date had pictured it in terms of local degeneracy. The decay of families and the sinking of communities into degeneracy had shocked and alarmed. This earlier literature concerned New England alone, and found the causes to be social. The Commission, of which Liberty H. Bailey was Chairman, pressed the inquiry deeper into the economic welfare of the people. They found the causes in the living conditions of the people, and

3

their summons has aroused all friends of the open country to work together for " better farming, better business, better living."

Writers and Proposed Remedies. This contrast between the early country life movement of New England and the present national country life movement is well expressed in the two books which may be called the best books on the subject. They are Anderson's *The Country Town,* published in 1906, two years before the Commission report was published, and Plunkett's *The Rural Life Problem in the United States,* published in 1910, two years after that momentous report was published. Each book is national in its message, though Anderson frankly wrote from a New England study window, and Sir Horace Plunkett from an Irish gentleman's country house : and each writer has grasped the fundamental processes of American rural life. But the last chapter of *The Country Town* pleads for " The Church as a Social Center "; while the message of *The Rural Life Problem* is that " There must be better farming, better business, and better living. These three are equally necessary, but better business must come first."   Dr. Anderson, out of the New England experience, alarmed by rural decay, summons us to social service, but Sir Horace Plunkett, from the experience of the Old World, and the wider investigation of American conditions, recognizes that the causes of rural decay are economic, and demands an initial economic remedy.

Four Types and Periods. The decay of rural

life in America is seen in four types: first individualism, second degenerate groups, third speculation, and fourth exploited lands. Each one of these is an enemy of the Church, and retards the growth of religion in the country. Each one of them arises, not out of the Church itself, but out of the social economy of the country. They are all results of causes which affect the farmer in the process of getting a living. Four periods of American country life are seen in these four kinds of decay: the pioneer, or solitary farmer; the land-farmer, or household farmer; the exploiter, or speculative farmer; and the husbandman, or organized farmer, who is fighting the present exploitation of land. These four great American countrymen have followed one another across the stage of the open country. They have built their churches and their communities like unto themselves. The spirit of the future is one of organizing the farmers and federating the churches. These types of men and communities have been successive. They appear in the order named. They are cumulative, and the later communities contain all the earlier types. The troubles with the country Church are those of transition from household farming to organized farming.

Individualist Phase. Individualism in American country life has been marked. Farmer folk will not combine, and they recognize few ties outside of a man's duty to himself. In the older settlements the farmer is very independent. He is not used to obeying any one, and he refuses to respond to commands from whatever quarter they may come. He follows leaders, and not principles. He looks upon the world as made up of persons, and nothing else. This individualism has been the blessing of the few and the bane of the many in New England, for it has caused the creation of a few bright and brainy people, while it has neglected great numbers of ordinary people. The degeneracy of the rural stock of New England in many places has been due to the selection of the favored individuals for emigration to the West and to the cities; and the abandonment of all the weaker members in the communities.[1]

Some of Its Effects. Individualism has been a factor in the dissolution of the rural household. The boy and girl have left home to seek a personal fortune. They have consulted personal pleasure rather than family advantage and have gone to the town or city to live, because there a better wage could be secured and more social pleasures enjoyed.

[1] The sensational picture by the Rev. Rollin Lynde Harte, which appeared in the *Atlantic Monthly,* Vol. LXXXIII, under the title "A New England Hill Town," and the article by President William DeWitt Hyde of Bowdoin College on the "Impending Paganism in New England," called public attention to the degenerate sections of New England. Dr. Josiah Strong pointed out in succeeding years the depletion of rural communities in States as far west as Illinois. Other writers depicted these processes, especially as they had roots in New England. An excellent summary of them is in the chapters on "The Extent of Rural Depletion" and "Local Degeneracy," in Dr. Wilbert L. Anderson's book, *The Country Town.*

The churches of the community have been multiplied by emphasis upon individual preference. Often one elderly church officer will insist upon the planting or the maintaining of a country church not needed in an overchurched community. Generally speaking, the problem of too many churches is due to the doctrine of personal salvation carried out to the extreme of personal selfishness. Yet the reason for the abuse is not in the doctrine, but in the circumstances under which they who believe that doctrine must needs work in getting a living.

A Deep-seated Evil. American life is still affected by pioneer days. The pioneer was lonely in his way of life, and he was lonely in his thoughts. He had to work and fight for himself. So he prayed for himself. Self-protection was his battle all day long, and soul salvation was his thought at night. He thought and wrought and fought all the week that he might survive, and on Sunday he craved only to hear how he might survive death. Other men have the same thought, but the pioneer had it to the exclusion of nearly all social feelings. The individualist has this exclusive care of his own soul, his own children, his own property, and his own pleasure. So deep-seated is this evil in American rural life that it is a foe to the progress of people in the open country. Coöperation and combination are nowadays the principles on which business success, educational advance, or religious efficiency are based. None of these is possible among farmers who are individualized. That which in pioneer days was a means of survival has become, in our time, a sign of retrograde living, and a cause of rural decay.

A Separating Force.   Here is the first clue to the mystery of overchurched communities.   The independence of pioneer days, once a noble trait, has become a base form of decay.   Generated in the solitary life of the woods, it has become a selfish philosophy in days long after the forests are gone. It makes country people suspicious of one another, and causes them to live in a sort of aggressive loneliness, the very opposite of a Christian state, and the active enemy of social service.

Household Group Phase.   The second form of rural decay is group degeneracy.   The second period of American rural life saw the perfecting of the household group.   From 1800 to 1890 the life on the farm was represented in the household perfection of Whittier's " Snowbound."   In those days the farmer was no longer living a lonely life.   He had neighbors, but his household was a complete unit in itself.   He had in his wife, children, and the grandparents, the maiden aunt of the family, and the hired man, a perfect little society.   The whole earth might in those days have been depopulated : and if there had been left one farmer's household in Ohio or New York, they could have repeopled the earth, and could have restored the arts, the religion, and the learning of mankind. The household farmer farmed the first values of the land which lay upon the surface.   He was not

PIONEER CABIN

PIONEER FAMILY

troubled with the depletion of the soil, the rotation of the crops, or the problem of nitrogen. He is the farmer of whom we think when we look back to the country life of the older days.

Weakened by Migration. This perfect group has suffered severely in the past twenty years. The church and the school, which are dependent upon it, have suffered with it. The picture at the World's Fair in Chicago entitled " Breaking Home Ties " depicted the crumbling of the family unit in the departure of the son from the farmhouse, never to return. The city has claimed a great share; and the West has enticed many away with its opportunities. They have gone, not as in earlier days, in families, compacted by common hardships, but person by person; and the family group in the country has been weakened by their migration.

Discouraged Remnants. Throughout much of New England the weakening of family life is evident. The depleted households cling to small and unproductive farms, by a fraction of their former strength. I remember driving, in my early ministry, from a prosperous farming section into a weakened community, whose lands had a lowered value because they lay too far from the railroad. My path to a chapel service on Sunday afternoon lay past seven successive farmhouses in each of which lived one member of a family, clinging in solitary misery to a small acreage which had a few years earlier supported a household. In that same neighborhood was one group of descendants

of two brothers, which had in two generations produced sixteen suicides. " They could not stand
trouble," the neighbors said. The lowered value of
their land, with consequent burdens, humiliation,
and strain, had crushed them. The very ability and
distinction of the family in the earlier period had the
effect, by contrast, to sink them lower down.

Persisting Primitive Types. There are families
in the older States which have preserved the simplicity and independence of the pioneer days. They
do not buy and sell, but the men make nearly everything needed for the household group. They live
in the simplicity of earlier days and by simplifying
their wants and multiplying their crafts they live
very near to the soil and very far from the world
market. You may call them degenerate. You may
call them primitive. The effect is the same. They
are not of the present. So far as the religious life of
the community is concerned they are aliens. A
primitive type which survives to a later day is essentially degenerate.

A Demoralizing Menace. A great deal of the
political trouble in the country towns of the eastern States is due to the buying and selling of votes.
Much of the difficulty in enforcing the laws against
the saloon is due to this alien and degenerate stock.
Dr. Wilbert L. Anderson has shown that the railroad
and the city have generally sifted out these weaker
members of the community. They have been carried into the city and sunk in the whirlpool of the
slum. It remains, however, for every New Eng-

land church to plan for the ministry which it can render to degenerate households, for the moral tone of the whole community is lowered by their presence. They are vessels filled with a bitter and poisonous liquor. They put the cup of impurity to the lips of the children of the cleanest families. The punishment of one member or the removal of another member of such groups as this does not end their virulent power for evil. A group, especially a household, has power to perpetuate itself, and these families are the waste of the noblest period in American agricultural history.

Speculative Phase. The third form of rural decay is the process of farm speculation. Speculation is a valuing of things in cash. It is an effort to " make money " without labor. In the household period of farming, about the '80s and '90s of the nineteenth century, country people began to value their property no longer as homes but as assets. A price was put upon the acre. The farm home was offered finally for sale. Remaining still a farmer, the man has moved to the westward, or to the eastward, from the central States, as the rising values of land have tempted him. The vicious and artificial character of his social life is evidenced by the fact that he has been profiting through the rising price of land in a time when the actual value of land is falling. An Illinois farmer told the writer, " I used to raise ninety bushels of corn per acre on my farm. I can now with better machinery only raise forty-five bushels per acre. At the same time my land has increased in value from thirty-five dollars per acre, when it was producing ninety bushels, to one hundred and fifty dollars per acre when it is producing forty-five bushels. The only thing that saved me was the rising price of farm products." This is a vicious and artificial system. While it is not all evil, it has left a deposit of speculative influence in the country. Churches and schools in the district in which this system of the speculative farmer prevails are weakened, the most of them are standing still, and the number of those which fail is as great as the number of those which are succeeding.

Effect of Abundant Cash. Rural decay through speculation shows itself in those regions in which the farmer sees before him a great profit through the sale of his properties and is transformed by this prospect into an idler. In southwestern Pennsylvania the farm lands are underlaid by beds of bituminous coal. The farmers of that section are of the household farming era. They have sold the coal under their land very generally and have received high prices for it. Sometimes the companies which now own the coal wait for years before mining it. Meantime, the farmers gradually have loosened and relaxed their methods of tilling the soil. After years of meager living they have come into possession of plenty of money. The older men maintain the industry of a lifetime, but imperceptibly the whole household, especially the younger members, show the corrupting influence of mere cash as

opposed to an economic system. The ministers of
that region and leading church people have come to
recognize the impending destruction of their
churches. They are praying and they are asking
for light as to the methods to be used in the era
just upon them.

Test of the Incoming Foreigners. As soon as the
coal company begins to operate its properties it
brings into the region great numbers of miners.
These men are foreigners. The bosses are from
the British Isles or from the older stock of immigrants. The miners themselves are from south-
eastern Europe, of those types of Europeans most
alien to American customs and institutions. No
severer strain can be put upon Christian institutions or upon public schools than such an invasion.
Weakened already by the decay of the speculative
process, these churches are ill prepared to minister
to the needy foreigner. They are too feeble to
teach the masterful industrial leaders their duty to
the poor and to the kingdom of God.

Question of Remedies. The remedy for this
decay is the exaltation of giving, when the farmers
first become rich, and the organizing of benevolence
through community enterprises. My purpose here
is to describe the process. The remedy is seldom
at hand. The trouble is that these changes through
speculation are too swift or their slow processes
are too subtle for religious men to understand
them, and to deal with them. The whole countryside
is often eaten with the social corrosion of the ex-

ploitation of land for coal, for iron, or other speculative commodities.

Exploitation Phase. The fourth form of decay is in the exploited lands and people. Farm life is like all other social life, subject to exploitation. Its values are seized by the masterful and by the selfish to increase their gains. The strong are made more powerful and the weak are ground into the earth. The country communities in all the eastern States show the effects of exploitation. They are almost hopelessly weakened through the depletion of the soil. In New England there are communities in which the land has been " ryed off." [1] Other towns have been exhausted by raising tobacco year after year without fertilization.

Example of Soil Exhaustion. Twenty years ago in Groton, Massachusetts, an old farmer, whose years and wisdom had earned him the title of " Uncle Rufus," took me to the top of a hill and pointing to the sandy stretches below us said, " Young man, you wouldn't believe that when I was your age I worked in fields of tobacco and of rye down there! We raised big crops there till there was no more in the soil. We never fertilized. Now that land only raises the scrub oak and stunted pine you see down there. It will never again be what it was."

Example of Missouri Town. In some parts of Missouri the community has been blighted by the transformation of farm land into mining land, and

[1] Land that has been robbed of its fertility by continuous crops of rye.

after the process is done there remains an impoverished stock, the leavings of a strong population,
who themselves ousted the farmer for the sake of
mineral wealth. Going on to other mining communities, they have left the weaker members of their
own households to fester socially and to decay
morally in a depleted and impoverished place. The
following quotation from the letter of an investigator in Missouri is a picture of such a mining town.
It shows the close relation between the impoverished
soil and the exploited people. It is a luminous illustration of the close relation between economic,
moral, and religious life. " It is a half-deserted
mining town. The reason it isn't all deserted is
because half the population were too lazy to move.
They lie around in dilapidated, unpainted, filthy
hovels from daylight to dark. There is a schoolhouse there : I mean there is a building there in
which children go to school. It is 25 by 50 feet in
size. It is frame ; several square yards of weather-
boarding have been torn from it; its door has been
kicked in. Of its ten windows six have been completely knocked out. Many panes of the remaining
four are broken. The blackboard is half demol-
ished. Some of the seats are torn loose. Filth is on
the floor. There is a road between Danforth and
Connellsville on which I had to walk my horse every
step. On the way I met another man on a horse.
He looked at me suspiciously and remarked that no
one ever traveled that road unless he was lost.
There are 4,766 people in this township. Less than

300 go to church; and the churches! Heaven help
them! Offering denominationalism and theology to
men who have practically no decent forms of social
gathering or recreation! The motion picture shows,
held in buildings fit only for kindling purposes, have
twice as many people in a night as the churches have
all week. These and the pool-rooms and Sunday
baseball games are the only places where men can
meet out of working hours."

Four Phases Summarized. One might summarize
this account of rural decay by saying that there
have been four successive types of countrymen, of
country community, and of country church in
America. These four are the solitary farmer, the
household farmer, the speculative farmer, and the
organized farmer.

Work with Present Forces. The repair of country life can only be made in modern terms. One
cannot rebuild the past. It is impossible to restore
the pioneer, much as his virtues are to be admired,
because he was made by the wild mountain and the
lonely prairie, which are no more. The household
organization of country life was created by a state of
affairs in which the household made all that it
consumed. It was complete in itself. This can
never come again, because the market to-day is the
world, and the farming class will not go back to
manufacturing all their necessities on their own
premises. We cannot restore the household type
of farming, though its moral and spiritual values
were very great.

EXTERIOR AND INTERIOR OF A COUNTRY SCHOOL
NO FOUNDATION, SIDING BROKEN, DOOR CRACKED

Scientific Farming the Basis. Scientific farming is the clue to the repair of country life. Not merely for profit, but for the building up of an intelligent organized country population, scientific agriculture will be of use in the country. It must be a gospel of the mind and soul, and on this new basis churches, schools, and whole communities will be erected.

Introduces New Method of Life. The beginning of this process is already made. The government of life in the country by scientific standards is accomplishing much. Farmers who are obliged to be scientific in order to raise any crop out of depleted soil are fighting the battle with adversity, using scientific agriculture as a military necessity. But when the necessity is past, they will have learned a new method of life. Sanitary reform is coming also in the country, based upon exact scientific research. Throughout the Southern mountains the hope is entertained by teachers and social workers that the campaign against the hook-worm will be successful. Already its results there are astonishing, and the victory against this enemy of social progress among Southern people is in sight, though far off.

Country Struggle Changing the South. The fight in the South against the boll weevil is proving a wonderful social discipline. It is organizing the people of the whole South to a sense of the value of science in the reorganization of country life. This victory is coming in two forms. It is compelling the farmer to till the crop with energy and precision. He can win a good crop by forced culture and reap it before the boll weevil has matured sufficiently to destroy it. But a greater discipline is felt throughout the South. The long-needed diversifying of Southern crops will come by the destruction of the cotton crop in some sections.

Approaching Farmer Organization. Corresponding to science as a discipline for agriculture, the organization of country people is necessary. Precisely as the labor unions have organized wage-earners, the farmers must organize. Not in the same terms nor with the same demands, but with equal thoroughness, and with the same subjection of the individual to the union of his fellows. These organizations which are now existing will have a variety of purposes. They are not merely for direct financial gain. So long as they go to the root of the farmer's prosperity, however, they will effect the same ethical and religious transformation. They will teach the farmer to coöperate and to obey. They prepare a way for the federation of the churches, and the unifying of every phase of country work.

A New Country Ideal. A new ideal of country life must arise out of the present struggle, and everywhere men are studying this ideal in the community. Its sources are in the experience of the older eastern States. New England was built under a community organization. The New England town is a self-governing community and the tradition of the Town Meeting has gone westward with a migrating population. Pennsylvania has in the Quakers and the Mennonites the community tradition in a more spiritual form. Disdaining the civil organization and caring nothing for politics, they formed themselves into communities by the genius of their religious system. They controlled the individual by methods of their own and coöperated in essential things for the common welfare.

Community in Action. The community is an old ideal, born out of the experiences of mankind in America and Europe, which expresses to-day the working principle of rural repair. The way to teach a population this ideal is not merely to preach it and to describe it, important as this is, but to practise it. People learn by what they do more than all that they hear. The first essential in teaching a community spirit is to organize a community act. Old Home Week in an eastern State will bring together a community meeting, and the effects of it will be illuminating to the minds of all. The celebration of the holidays of the year has power to awaken the community spirit, if this celebration is in common for all. It is not enough to have a Thanksgiving service in the church. Indeed, such a meeting may be a denial of community principles. But the celebration of Christmas, Easter, Memorial Day, Fourth of July, Labor Day, and Thanksgiving should be so public and should be in such terms that the whole population will respond. The custom of so doing, even though it recurs but twice a year, will have amazing power in organizing a community sense.

Preacher as Community Leader. The community leader is an organizer. Therefore the preacher or teacher should get his people to do the things which he wants them to believe. For infallibly action precedes thought, but when he has started the practise of the community he must not fail to state the ideal to the community. He must keep before their minds a constructive, consistent community organization. This will have persuasive influence over those who are practising the thing itself. Little by little the ideal in its mental forms will strike into their hearts, mellowed and prepared by the enterprises and the enjoyments of community practise. The business of the preacher is to state the ideals arising in the experience of the people.

Emphasis on Country Values. The repair of country life will come in those forms which give value to the things in the open country. The community must move and breathe in joy and enthusiasm of the country. The celebrations must be of country matters, not those of the city. It must arise as far as possible on the ground, and must be essential to the life of people living in the open country. In this way the country community will mark out its own path of growth and progress. It will have life of its own of which it will soon boast, and the streams of waste will be stopped. The exodus from the country will be turned back and the community will be built.

CHURCH AND COMMUNITY

Nevertheless, the Church has a peculiarly close relationship to the other rural institutions, and in fact to all the movements of rural life. The Church has not adequately appreciated this fact, which has its origin in a characteristic feature of country life; namely, that all its interests are very intimately bound together. The work of the farm and of the household, the life of the family, the amusements of the neighborhood, the interests of all in school, Grange, and Church are closely intertwined.—*K. L. Butterfield*

This ideal of a Church which makes itself a factor in building up a community, even in material things, is not an impossible ideal. It has been realized in the past and it can be realized again. An illustrious example is that of John Frederic Oberlin, the pastor of the Steinthal. Numberless other examples can be found in the religious orders of the medieval Church,—examples of communities which were made rich and prosperous by the teachings and the example of self-sacrificing leaders. This ideal will, however, never be realized by a Church which affects to despise this world and the things of this world, which regards the world itself as lost, and conceives of its own mission as consisting in saving as many individual souls as possible from the wreck.

If the Church will assume that the world is not going to perdition, that it is going to last for a long time, and that it will eventually be a Christian or a non-Christian world, according as Christians or non-Christians prove themselves more fit to possess it—according as they are better farmers, better business men, better mechanics, better politicians—then the Church will turn its attention more and more to the making of better and more progressive farmers, business men, mechanics, and politicians.—*Thomas Nixon Carver*

II

CHURCH AND COMMUNITY

Close Relationship. The country church is married to the country community. That which affects the one affects also the other. If the community is impoverished, the church wears a pinched appearance. If the community is prosperous, the church under normal conditions shows growth and self-respect.

Church Shows Community Condition. The country church is the weather vane of community prosperity. It is a voluntary institution, divinely given as an index of how well the farmer is getting on. The tilling of the soil is an occupation which cannot be carried on except by sober men, and it has never been maintained in a population through succeeding generations except among religious people. The relation between work and worship is more evident in the country than in the city, for rural life is simple and its social texture is clear to the observer. The working of cause upon effect is plain in the country. There are not so many disturbing or extraneous forces and there are but few interferences between cause and effect. The bearing of economic life upon religious institutions is much more evident than in the city, because country life is highly organized, but simple.

Community Defined. What is a community? A man or woman in the country lives his whole life within the radius of a team haul from his home. However much he visits without this circle, his knowledge of the community is one hundred times more intense and personal than his knowledge of any other community. In this small republic to which he is limited by the common means of transportation, he visits, he buys and sells, he worships, he marries, and within this radius he buries his dead.

Common View. This enables one to define the community in popular terms, as a child might define it, as " the place where we live." This includes locality, personal and social relations, and vital experience. The community is the larger whole in which the members of a we-group find satisfaction of their vital needs. This means that the community is the virgin soil of the Kingdom. The Church when it pervades the whole life of the community constitutes with it a little republic of God, because the whole life of the people in that community is lived within this range.

Another Definition. Another definition of a community is given by Professor Charles A. Elwood.[1] " A society is, therefore, a group of people living together by means of interstimulation and response.

[1] Charles A. Elwood, of the University of Missouri, in *American Journal of Sociology,* March, 1911, p. 835.

What its total life is depends very largely upon the attitude of its members toward one another. How they coöperate depends, therefore, upon common will, belief, and opinion, and the agencies by which common will, belief, and opinion effect social control. These agencies are chiefly religion, government and law, and education."

Church as Community Center. The Church, because of its relation to the community, should be a community center. It can not exist and prosper unless it is the focus of the life of the community. Now communities are of infinitely varied size and form. They are not perfect circles or squares or ellipses. They cannot be brought down to any geometrical terms. One uses the word " center " as a suggestive term, because there is no better. If the church, being vitally connected with the community, does not make itself central to the life of the community, it will not continue to exist. There may be several such centers in a community, but their relation to the whole people must in some way be vital, or they will pine and die.

Individualist Churches. The churches of individualist communities have served their people by ministering to persons alone. Their method is the preaching of sermons. They have no other. The typical man in pioneer and settler days was an individualist. He was made such by his work and by the lonely struggle of his life. He could be no other than what God, by means of the forest, the vast open prairie, and the lonely work at the furrow, made him. His wife spent her solitary hours over the varied occupations of the primitive household, and she too was a strong, resourceful individual. She had but few social traits as compared with the modern woman. The church that ministered to such people could preach a gospel of individual salvation alone. It would have been false to its duty if it had preached any other. It needed no methods such as our later churches use. It had the one method: the periodic revival of religion for individual souls.

Call for the Emotional. For the individualist is a man of warm heart, of passionate interest, of devoted friendships, and resolute loyalty. To him life means nothing but persons. Therefore the church of settler folk and the church which has pioneer individuals in any numbers in its membership must use emotional methods. Of course if you do not care to win and to hold this kind of people, you can omit the measures by which they are to be won; but these measures are always emotional, because the emotional, individual type of Christian is produced by his occupation and by his inheritance. He can be only what he is. He must be dealt with in his own terms. Country people are very many of them pioneers. The number of pioneers is greater among the older people than among the younger; but for some time to come the country Church will have to deal with the proud, solitary, and passionate personalities of men who can be won and can be served by their feelings alone.

"All Day Sings." In some parts of Alabama, conspicuously in the sandy stretches of the lower Appalachian Mountains, the people have a custom known as " all day sings." Certain singing masters make a business of going through the country and collecting the folk on Sundays for singing. These men have a rough and effective power in song. They use generally no instrument and therefore the rhythm and the swing of the music are its most notable elements. For hours the people sit under the leadership of the singing master and sing simple, popular, religious songs. Little by little the master selects those whom he calls his school. They are the best singers and he keeps them in permanent connection with himself, coming back again to that community for later performances.

Suggestion to Churches. The churches through all this country have learned that people will not go to church within a radius of several miles of an " all day sing." Sunday-schools have to be closed and church services are but little attended. Yet families will drive ten miles to the " all day sing " and spend the whole Sunday, eating their meals in the intervals between sessions and driving home at night, every way content. These gatherings are the expression of the overflowing emotionalism of the people of that country. It would seem that the churches there could use the method which has grown out of the life of the people and make effective for their own use what is a matter of private profit to the singing masters.

Extreme Church Individualism. The church in settler days, when every one is highly individualized, is scarcely to be called an institution. Its building is a mere roof over a pulpit. Its work consists of preaching and no more. It has no societies or organizations. The settler and the pioneer would believe it wicked to organize the societies which an ordinary village church of our day thinks necessary. Among the Southern mountains, where the pioneer type, strongly individualized, remains, where every man is an independent person and every woman is a strong character, the churches have but one method of religion; namely, the periodic revival. They think the methods of the people in the valley to be wicked, unreligious, and expressive of unregenerate minds. To them Ladies' Aid societies are unspiritual, Sunday-schools are sinful, and boys' clubs are extremely worldly.

Ministry to Pioneers. In every church of modern times there remain some pioneers. The settler has come down through later generations. The individualist is a factor and he must be dealt with in his own terms. It is not fair for him to tyrannize over others any more than it is right for others to exact of him what he cannot furnish. Teach him the gospel of personal salvation, for religion means personal things to him, and these alone. Arouse him with emotion. Attach him to persons. Teach him to command and to obey those whom he loves, but do not expect in his own life to change him into another type, for that is impossible. Ministers who are serving in communities of settlers, of pioneers and mountaineers, have a great duty of evangelism. If they cannot preach a gospel that moves the heart, they had better go elsewhere. If they cannot live a life that grips the heart and holds the affections, they can accomplish nothing among a people dominated by emotion.

Man by Man Work. The community life of the individualist type is a mere aggregate. However closely the people in it are related to one another, they are a mere heap of separate units. They are not an organism growing together and knit into one by organized vital relations. In the West in new settlements every man is equal to every other, and pure democracy prevails. In the Southern mountains each man stands on his own acres and faces the world without fear. He extends the hospitality of his house with the grace of a great lord. He avenges his own injuries with his own hand. His mode of life has made him solitary and independent. He is ready at a moment's notice to quarrel with his nearest kinsman and to carry the feud through the years of his life. These are the signs of a religion of personal salvation. Where these signs appear, personal work, the preaching of the gospel, the ministry of man to man, are the only forms in which the Church can serve the community. Such a thing as social service, the ministry of a consecrated man to a society, is almost impossible. The people must here be dealt with man by man and that which wins the one has no influence upon the other. The conquest of one heart does not lead to the conquest of the neighbor's heart.

Period of the Household Type. The second type which has appeared in America is the household farmer. The Church represents the life of the people and is as faithful to the household type as to the pioneer. That is its duty under God. This type of church and community is more general throughout the country, for the household tillage of the land has been the most general type of agriculture in America. In Illinois this type of farming became general about 1835 and its period ended about 1890. In the Eastern States, Massachusetts and New York, the days of the settler whose farming was individualist ended about 1800, and the household farmer possessed the land until about 1890. The beginning of the household farming period was in the perfection of the family group. The end of it is indicated by the appearance of abandoned farms, renters or tenants in the country, and landlords living in the towns.

Its Practise and Ideals. The household farmer owned his land, and tilled it for the first values of the soil. He had neighbors and knew how to treat them kindly, to marry his children to their children, to exchange with them many social and helpful services, but he did not coöperate with them in economic welfare. The household farmer competed with his neighbors in getting his income, while the modern farmer coöperates with his neighbors in the securing of a livelihood. Above all, the household

farmer perfected the family group. His household became the type of American life. The ideals
of all American morality, of right feeling and of
religion, were the outgrowth of household farming.

Its Church Life. The Church of the household
farmer expressed, as did the community, his mode
of life. Unlike the Church of individualists, it possessed a place for the children in the Sunday-
school, even for the infants in the primary department. It perfected societies for women long before
a woman's club movement gave them a new enjoyment. It organized young people's societies, which
in the '80s and '90s blossomed forth in the Young
People's Society of Christian Endeavor and kindred
national movements. The country Church of the
household type had even some organizations for
boys, though these were uncommon. This type of
Church is distinctly unlike that which preceded it.
in the wealth of its recognition of family life.
Central to its whole organization was the family
pew.

Facing Changed Conditions. This is the country
Church of which we have thought in the past. It is
this country Church which has suffered in recent
years, and whose weakness has attracted the attention of religious thinkers. Just as the pioneer
Church, with its individualist preaching and its
one method of periodic revival, was succeeded by
the household Church, whose methods are many
and whose various organizations would have seemed
to the pioneer sinful, so the country Church of the

household farming era is being transformed into a new type, because the community of household farmer has since 1890 undergone transformation. The first business of the devout Christian in the country Church is to recognize this inevitable change and to foresee the type into which the Church is to be transformed.

Good Features Conserved. Meantime, the country Church of the household farmer is the type of Church still remaining in many parts of the country. It is important for us to recognize the services and the work of this Church, and to indicate the ways by which it can serve the country community. It is important also to remember that in the future the new type of Church will possess all the good traits of those which have gone before. Just as the household farming Church retains the preaching of the gospel of personal salvation and the periodic revival of religion—a religion of the heart—so the Church of the newer type that is to come will preserve these individualist and primitive customs, because they are good, along with every good custom of the household farmers' Church.

Different Conditions in Canada. Conditions in Canada are strikingly different from those in the United States. Among country churches the predominant type of Church is that of the household farmer. Three reasons explain this. Much of the country has been settled later than parts of the United States on the same parallels of longitude. Secondly, the Canadians are more tenacious, and

slower to change. The third reason is the settlement, in the eastern provinces, of many Scotch
people, and kindred types, who, as will be shown
elsewhere, have demonstrated their ability to resist
the changes I am describing. All this is for the
good of Canadian Christianity. The later and more
deliberate settlement will make possible the assimila-
tion of later experience and of a more mature
Christian sociology. The general conservatism, if
it be wise, can retain the best of the old, while making ready for the new. And the genius of certain
national stocks will strengthen the national fiber
against destructive change.

General Canadian Movement. It is therefore the
general task of Canadian Christians, so far as they
differ from their brethren in the States, to build the
Church upon the family group. For there will not
be a long pioneer period in any part of Canada.
The fine family life of those communities which
have begun to disintegrate in the States will last
for decades longer in many parts of Canada. It
is to be hoped that, without impairment of this
group-life in the churches, the newer social order
may be taught to the people. For the latter stages
of country life will come. The destination of all
American farming is in the direction of what I
have called " husbandry." Conservatism can only
postpone it; and happy that conservatism which
sees in the mistakes of the more swiftly moving
" States " the sign-posts of its own future course.

Source of Religious Competition. The Church is

made up of households, as the community is made up of farmhouses. It is a dignified assembly of groups. Its spirit is one of neighborliness, but not of coöperative unity. The farmers have kindly and genial relations with one another: their social pleasures are from common sources. They intermarry, they borrow and they lend, but they are not unified in their farming. In social life they are one: in business life they are many. In business affairs through the working day they compete: and the result is that the Church of households teaches religious competition and division; because religious institutions are determined in their form by economic experience. In his economic experience the household farmer is his neighbor's opponent and competitor.

Lacking in Community Feeling. This explains why there are so many churches in the country. The land-farmer lived and worked for his own household. It seemed to him no ill that his neighbor should not be in the same church. He had no conception of the community as the basis of common welfare. His basis of living is his farm. It matters not to him if his neighbor's farming fails. He has rather a pleasant feeling in his own success and in the contrast to his neighbor's loss. If his orchard has a good crop he has no regret that his neighbor's orchard has none, knowing that the price of apples may be higher. His whole life is lived in competition with those outside of his own household group. The result is that his religious life is an

experience of competition, except with the group of
households who are within his own congregation.

Traditional Competitive View. The household
farmer believes that country churches are maintained by competition, and this view prevails in
many high places. Leaders among all Protestant
churches hold with respect the view that " If you
take the Methodist Church out of the neighborhood,
the Presbyterian Church will die." This view is
traditional. It comes out of the household farmers'
way of life. It may have had truth during the era
of household farming, but it is based on no co-
operative principle. Communities cannot be built
out of competition : they must be dominated by
union.

Impressive and United Worship. The churches
of the household era of farming have been inspiring
and noble institutions. The Church as an institution grew up in the country in this time, for the
earlier church of the pioneer could scarcely be
called an institution. The gathering of farmers in
their substantial vehicles from far and near on the
Sabbath morning was a spectacle which deeply impressed the casual visitor, or the hired man as
he came into the community. I confess that no
scene stirs my heart more deeply than the sight of
many horses and carriages standing about the country church, the horse-sheds full, every tree a hitch-
ing-post, and rows of riding-horses and carriage
animals tethered to the fences : these all give an impression of the assembled community. The quiet

exterior of the meeting is in vivid contrast to its intense and thronged interior. The dignified voice of the preacher or the solemn joining in the hymn, complete the impression of the whole community assembled in church. Each man sits with his family and the mother with her children. The young men and women, while seated apart, are in the liveliest emotional consciousness of one another; and the choir, well aware of their importance in the service, are in their place. The preacher, who sees less of his people than of the unseen realities of which he is to testify, feels that upon him rests the meaning of the whole occasion. But in that audience every man has his own thoughts and every household present is as significant in its attendance upon worship as the household of the preacher. Such a country church is an assemblage of homes. It is a great symbol of social unity.

Present Speculative Influence. The third type of communities in the country is the speculative. American country life is now undergoing the corrosive influence of exploitation. The values of land are swiftly changing over the whole United States. The day of household farming is closing. Few territories exhibit the household farmer as the dominant type throughout a whole population. In most of the States, even in the South, speculation in land has brought into the community the three figures, represented in many individuals, whose influence is greater upon the Church and community than that of any minister of religion. These three are the renter or tenant farmer, the retired farmer, and the landlord. Their participation in country life has wholly changed household farming into a new type. This process is not yet completed, but the present distress and weakness of country churches is a sign of its transforming influence in country life.

Money Valuing of Land. Exploitation is the turning of other values into money. It is not mere speculation, though in many communities the exploitation of farm land has brought into existence land speculators. In a Western farming community, I am told, the process of speculation has gone so far that the town supports a real estate agent for every thousand acres of land which is open to the buying and selling. This, however, is extreme. The usual process is one in which the farmer, who once thought of his property as a home, now thinks of it in terms of dollars and cents. The land-farmer, or household farmer, had no price upon his land. He did not know what it was worth. He did not usually know how much his income was. But gradually, in the years of migration, the farmers in the more progressive and central States, such as Illinois and Ohio, began to value their land and their homes in terms of money.

Period of Exploitation. This must have been in the older and eastern States a bitter process, for on the land-farmer's acres were buried the ashes of his ancestors for two or three generations. The household farmer had consecrated his land by set-

ting God's acre in the corner of the field. The day
came after the Civil War, with the realization that
the first values of the land were exhausted, when
the household farmer set off for the West. He sold
or abandoned his land, on which his ancestors had
lived, and began that emigration to the West which
has characterized the last forty years. In these
forty years farm lands have been exploited, bought
and sold by farmers themselves. The prices of
land at first slowly, but of late very swiftly, have
increased. In the past ten years in the Middle West
this increase has been in some sections about one
hundred per cent.[1]

Giving as a Timely Message. The churches of
speculative farmers are churches whose most marked
characteristic is giving. We are likely to think of
speculation as a purely destructive process. It is
the acid bath in which the farmer's social economy
is dipped, which burns off all that is not permanent
in the previous economy, and prepares for the putting on of the new order in which the farmer shall
till the land by science rather than by tradition. But
speculation is a process of valuing things in cash.
The Church, as all other things, comes to be estimated in terms of money. The doctrine of the
exploiter is the doctrine of giving. This is the transformation which country churches need to make at
the present time. Other things in the country community are valued in money. The farmer has been

[1] Professor John Lee Coulter in the *Statistical Journal,*
March, 1911.

RENTER'S BARN AND CABIN

eager for cash with which to secure better machinery, suitable fertilizers for his land, education for his children, and other aids to progress. He is eager to use money in preparing himself for the new era into which he is going, and he is perfectly right. It is important that religion be interpreted to him in terms of giving money. The consecration of wealth is the doctrine which the minister must preach to farmers in the day of buying and selling.

Program of Improvements. The country community is profoundly affected in like manner by speculation. The problems of the community come to be those of new taxation for better schools, bonding the county for the construction of stone roads, and securing contributions for libraries, for the organizing of Young Men's Christian Associations, and other projects which call for cash. The old-fashioned farmer resists these demands. He is not accustomed to spending large monies upon public projects. He is suspicious of bonds and of all investments in anything which he cannot see. The pioneer or settler farmers sturdily resist these interpretations of the community in terms of cash. But the leaders of the community see that the process which puts a price upon an acre, which compels the old-fashioned farmer to sell the dust of his ancestors, has been inspired by God and is necessary in the life of a growing community.

Exploitation a Brief Transition Era. It is probable that the period of exploitation is but temporary. Professor Ross [1] describes the period of exploitation as a mere dawning of the day of scientific farming. It would bring great hope and encouragement to country ministers who suffer from the effects of speculation in farm land to know that this day is but short. Most important of all is it that they should know what to do in this time of transition. The task of the minister and of other community leaders is expressed in one word: the consecration of private wealth to the use of the community.

Aims for the Country Worker. In another place the methods of raising money for religious uses will be dealt with. Here we are only interested in urging the worker in the country to see that his relation to these public enterprises is twofold: first, to arouse a spirit of public willingness to give and to pay; second, to watch with critical eye these investments by taxes and all bond issues, in order to insure honesty and to distribute the burden with justice and fairness upon the present and upon future generations.

Teach Doctrine of Giving. A new standard of expenditure must be attained in the country. It is the business of the religious leader in the country, more than of any other person, to teach the farmers who are prospering in cash values the doctrine of giving. The nature of the community and the intensified value of the community's institutions must

[1] "Agrarian Changes in the Middle West," *American Journal of Economics,* December, 1910.

be made clear to country people, and a spirit too of sharing the prosperity which God has given must be imparted to them. This spirit above all is religious.

Beginnings of Organization Era. The fourth type of Church and community in the country is based upon organized or scientific farming, which is the destination of American agriculture. Churches of this type are few. Communities of organized farming are, except on the Pacific Coast, still fewer. Individual farmers who are tilling their land by science are many, but their total number in comparison to the population of the country as a whole is very small. They usually constitute but a fraction of any community except in particular territories.

Marked Characteristics. Organized farming presents certain marked characteristics. These marks are seen in the churches of husbandmen and in the communities in which they live. For the mode by which the people of the country get their living is the organizing factor in religious and in community life.

Dependence upon Scientist. The first of these characteristics is the dependence of the farmer upon the scientist. The tillage of the soil by the household group was traditional. Lessons were taught by the father to the son; by the old man to the young. Its weakness was in its inability to meet new situations and its lack of resources after the first values of the soil were exhausted. The scientific farmer goes to the university for his methods. He reads the bulletins of the State and national departments. He attends the farmers' institute. He does his own thinking in greater measure than any countryman who preceded him, because he has more to think about. He has, if necessary, the analysis of his soil, and he frankly recognizes the dependence of his agriculture upon the scientific man. This dependence is as close as the relation of the operating surgeon to the investigator and diagnostician. It follows that the scientific farmer cannot teach his own son in the present generation. The son who comes home from college may even teach his father, if the father be intelligent enough to appreciate the modern learning relating to the farm.

Principle of Coöperation. In the second place, scientific farming tends to be coöperative. The competition of household groups with one another disappears in the face of the common struggle to gain a market. Long ago Hesiod, the Greek poet, discovered that agriculture is coöperative by its very nature. It has taken American farmers a long time to discover this fact, by comparing the experience of different sections. Those farmers whose churches and communities have survived the destructive period of speculation in land are all strengthened by coöperation in some thorough form. The new coöperative tillage of the Maryland Eastern shore, of Kentucky, and of Oregon, which is described in the chapter on " Coöperation and

Federation," is an application of this principle announced by Hesiod eight centuries before Christ that farming is coöperation. The coöperative organizations of farmers are the greatest moral force in controlling the individual and imposing upon him standards of justice, fairness, self-sacrifice, and obedience.

Use of Marginal Values. The third characteristic of scientific farming is the use of marginal values. The land-farmer in the nineteenth century lived by the values which lay on the top of the ground, abundant fertility of soil, rich resources in timber, unexploited mines of coal, iron, mica, or copper. The farmer who must organize to get a living makes his profit from the by-products. He must till the soil so that its fertility is retained and increased. He cannot afford to waste, for he is dealing with a depleted and weakened soil. The religious and moral character of the new era in agriculture is seen in this struggle of the farmer to live, not by first values, but by final values of the soil, of the wood-lot, and of his own energies.

Example of Such Values. Marginal values are those by which the milk farmer lives, who maintains his farm and his establishment by milking forty to seventy cows. But these bring him no profit. In the middle of the day, " between chores," he tills a piece of land on which perhaps he raises a crop; which he sells for cash. This crop is clean gain. It is his marginal labor. It is done with the unemployed hours of his man and himself. The dairy keeps up the fertility of the soil and pays the bills of the farm, but the extra crop of the orchard brings in a clean, undiminished profit.

Church Becomes a Community Center. The Church of the organized farmer is an organized Church. Dr. Edward Judson, in New York, defines the institutional Church as " organized kindness." The country Church which ministers to scientific farmers might be called organized social life; for social life generates religion and exhibits Christian experiences. The Church of the scientific farmer, therefore, should be a local agency of the kingdom of God. It should embody in itself the whole community. It should be a community center.

Community Like One Household. For it is obvious that with the coming of organized farming the community has taken the place of the household. It is indeed a large household. No longer do households compete with one another, for the farmers who are organized compete with all the rest of the world through a coöperative association in which they are all members. Thus the country people who till the soil by science become closely compacted and intimately related to one another. In the old time the household farmer taught his son how to farm. His wife taught her daughter how to cook and to sew. These processes are now taught in the community by the teacher of agriculture and the teacher of domestic science. The farmer sits side by side with his son on the bench in the grange hall or in the church parlors to hear a lecture and demonstration by a scientific farmer. The classroom becomes an essential part of the process of agriculture and it is a community classroom.

Community Service of the Sunday-school. In the same manner religion is taught in the organized farming community in the Sunday-school. In the old days it was taught in the household. Among the best families, and most devout, religion will continue to be taught at the fireside, and worship will culminate in the family altar, but the family altar and fireside are inadequate to the religious problem of a community in which men's lives are compacted into a social whole. For, in intense social life, it is as important to educate your neighbor's children as it is to educate your own. The devout farmer soon learns that the children of his hired man are a bigger influence upon his own children than he is himself. In order to preserve the religious tradition in his own house, he must bring up the children of his neighbor to his own standards; hence the Sunday-school becomes the community institution which bears up the whole task of religious education. The farmer takes his place as teacher of a Bible class. His influence on his own sons is exerted when they come to him in their turn with the sons of other men to be taught what he is best qualified to teach. His wife becomes the teacher of the primary department and all the children of the community come to her, including her own. Through this department she teaches in the community much better than she could teach in her own home.

Religious Education Centralized.   Religion itself, as understood to-day, cannot be taught in the household.   Modern pedagogy and the methods of teaching which are used in the schools and colleges can be adopted by Sunday-schools, but cannot be adopted by firesides.   Most parents are incapable of teaching in the terms of modern religious education.   For this reason the Sunday-school becomes the community center in religious education.   All the children of the countryside—not merely the children of church-members—can be brought together and thus assemble for learning at the feet of Jesus Christ.   The community has become the home of the individual, and in that home every child and every man has the influence upon every other which the members of a household once had in the earlier days upon other members.

SCHOOLS FOR COUNTRY LIFE

But if this attraction—the attraction of common work and social intercourse with a circle of friends—is to prevail in the long run over the lure which the city offers to eye and ear and pocket, there must be a change in rural education. At present country children are educated as if for the purpose of driving them into the towns. To the pleasure which the cultured city man feels in the country— because he has been taught to feel it—the country child is insensible. The country offers continual interest to the mind which has been trained to be thoughtful and observant; the town offers continual distraction to the vacant eye and brain. Yet, the education given to country children has been invented for them in the town, and it not only bears no relation to the life they are to lead, but actually attracts them toward a town career.—*Horace Plunkett*

The subject of paramount importance in our correspondence and in the hearings is education. In every part of the United States there seems to be one mind, on the part of those capable of judging, on the necessity of redirecting the rural schools. There is no such unanimity on any other subject. It is remarkable with what similarity of phrase the subject has been discussed in all parts of the country before the commission. Everywhere there is a demand that education have relation to living, that the schools should express the daily life, and that in the rural districts they should educate by means of agriculture and country-life subjects. It is recognized that all difficulties resolve themselves in the end into a question of education.— *Report of the Country Life Commission*

The simple organization of the Sabbath-school makes it peculiarly fitted for the special service it has rendered in the rural parts of our land. As a force for the evangelization of urban and rural life it is greater than it has been at any previous time. There are two phases of Sabbath-school work: the first is an evangelizing agency in places where no local church exists; the second is as a part of the regular work of an established local church. In the first, it is a pioneer; in the second, it is "the Bible-studying-and-teaching service of the Church."

The Sabbath-school has been described as "the most flexible, adaptable, and far-reaching institution ever designed for the conversion of the world." The Sabbath-school in its missionary phase has been one of the chief forces for the evangelization of new-country communities, and the pioneer of the Church on the frontier. Missionaries, churches, and redeemed communities throughout the land testify to the efficiency of this popular and rational method of evangelization.—*J. O. Ashenhurst*

48

III

SCHOOLS FOR COUNTRY LIFE

Religious Inspiration Needed. Nothing short of religious devotion will organize an adequate educational system for the whole people. The common school system, based on the purpose to educate all the children of a commonwealth, was launched in Scotland and in New England at the close of the seventeenth century, under intense and masterful religious devotion. We are confronted with a task as great in the need of adequate education in country communities in America. The common schools, the Sunday-schools, and the extension departments of agricultural colleges are in need of a new inspiration. They will receive it only from sources which are essentially religious.

Reconstruction in Denmark. The recent experience of Denmark illustrates this thesis.[1] In forty years Denmark has been reconstructed as a nation, lifted out of the depression of a great military defeat, out of debt, and out of social disorganization. This has been accomplished by the schoolmasters of Denmark. Serious observers attribute the central, inspiring influence to the folk high schools, estab-

[1] See Appendix A.

lished as a religious enterprise by Bishop Grundtvig and his associates.

Value of Rural Schools. The one-room rural schools which prevail in the country have been of enormous influence in American life. Their organization as a system was one of the greatest educational tasks in history. For they were planted by an advancing tide of immigration as a new continent was being peopled. One marvels at the statesmanship which maps out a vast region on the scale of the short legs of a six-year-old child, for the school district is standardized by the ability of a little child to walk morning and night to and from school.

Present Diminished Usefulness. But wonderful as the one-room school system is, with the passing of the household farming era its usefulness rapidly diminishes. It was established at the close of the pioneer period. As communities were formed in the beginning of settled social life, this school was at its highest value. While the rural household was complete unto itself and while the economic skill of the country was imparted from the father to the son, it was not necessary for the country schools to be strong. They needed only to be universal, simple, elastic, and systematic. The " three R's " were sufficient as an education for those whose real training for life was in the home and imparted by tradition from parent to child.

Call for Reorganization. But with the coming of scientific farming and the reorganization of country life, the one-room rural schools need to be reorganized. They have already lost the enthusiastic support which they once had from the farmer. Organized and scientific farmers do not find themselves served as well by the one-room school as their fathers did in the household farming era. Instead of insisting upon the "three R's" alone, the organized farmer is eagerly seeking for industrial training. The country school, therefore, has no longer the same settled place in his mind. A rural investigator in northern Missouri reports that in thirty miles of travel on country roads he saw not one house or barn unpainted, but every schoolhouse out of repair. The farmers are building up everything but the country schools. The one-room rural school is no longer to them a serviceable institution. These grown-up farmers are assembling regularly to learn in middle life the reasons of scientific agriculture, but the schoolhouse and the schoolteacher are not a part of this new system.

Work of Recent Writers. It should be borne clearly in mind that this lack in the country school affects the religion of the country community, and with equal clearness it should be remembered that the change in the value of the country school comes with the introduction of speculation into agricultural life. When the farming of a region goes through a rapid increase in values of land, when tenant farmers invade a neighborhood in large proportion, when the farm landlord comes to be a notable figure in agriculture, and when farmers retire to the towns to live, then the country schools need to be revised in the interest of the farmer, the school-teacher, and the country Church. The books on the country school are at the present time among the best books for reading among religious people. No writer or speaker in the country is more stimulating to a church audience than Professor H. W. Foght of Kirksville, Missouri, whose book, *The American Rural School,* illuminates the problem of the American rural Church. The writings and publications of Superintendent O. J. Kern,[1] of Winnebago County, Illinois, are of great value to those who would understand country life. Miss Mabel Carney is a writer and speaker on country life, whose insight and comprehension of the school question have qualified her to speak with equal force to the country minister. She has been a valuable helper in many conferences and schools for country ministers. These leaders in the reconstruction of country schools illustrate in their service to the country Church the unity of the rural problem. Country life is simple. That which is true of one institution in the country holds for the others. The process which changes the mind of the countryman, in his thought of his schools, will alter and elevate his thought of the Church; and all these changes of the rural mind are dependent upon changes in economic and social experience.

Proposed Improvements. These writers on the

_____
[1] *Among Rural Schools,* and *Annual Report of Winnebago County Schools.*

MODEL RURAL SCHOOL, KNOX COUNTY, MISSOURI

American rural school believe in the improvement
of the one-room country school, in a living salary
for the teachers, in adequate and professional supervision of country schools, and in the consolidation
of very many country schools, independent of town
or village. The important principle in all these
proposed changes is the service of the country
school to the working farmer. The changes needed
are those which will make the school serviceable
in the task which the farmer has to perform;
namely, the industrial struggle by which he gets
his living, and the social reorganization by which
he shall live on a higher modern plane, after he
has got a better income. In other words, the rural
schools are called on to respond to the challenge,
"better farming, better business, better living."

Place Still for One-room Schools. It is not
necessary to go into technical details here as to improvement of schools in the country. The reader
had better look to those who are school authorities
themselves for these details, but I believe that the
one-room country school will in many places permanently survive. There are isolated valleys and
hilly or mountainous plateaus or lonely districts in
which the country school must be small and one
teacher will be adequate to the needs of the few
children in the place. There is much to be said
for the one-room school, provided it has a good
equipment and a devoted, well-trained teacher.
Let us suppose, therefore, that in a fertile mountain valley there are twenty children in a popula-

tion not likely to be increased. What improvements are necessary to make the school a part of the vital reorganization of the country?

Adequate Teacher's Salary.   First of all, the teacher should have an adequate salary, and, whatever payment is necessary by the State or by the district, it must be sufficient to sustain a self-respecting man or woman through a whole year. This is the basis of permanent teaching. Our school in the valley will not prosper, if it is not able to retain a teacher, once selected, who serves the needs of the neighborhood. Without at least three years of consecutive, devoted service by a teacher any country school will be inefficient. No teacher can become a part of the vital organization of a district, if he does not stay there for year after year, and no country school district can select its teacher without the leverage of an adequate salary. If the teacher, moreover, has to work at something else in vacation, if he has not a sufficient living to attend summer schools and improve year by year in school and pedagogic wisdom, the school will retrograde. Therefore the salary of the teacher must be adequate for a year's living.

Adequate Supervision.   Secondly, there is need in the open country of adequate supervision of the common schools. Except in New England, where in some States the supervision is by farmers, every State has county superintendents of schools. But the county unit is too large for one man to cover. One superintendent in Illinois has a territory so

CENTRALIZED SCHOOL, INDIANA

CENTRALIZED SCHOOL, OHIO

large that it would require forty days, and seven hundred and twenty-two miles of travel, to visit the schools for which he is responsible. Moreover, adequate supervision should be by trained teachers. At present the superintendent may or may not be a teacher, but he must be a politician. It would be better for the supervisors of the county to appoint the superintendent than for the voters to elect him. For the training of these superintendents there should be special courses provided. These measures would give adequate supervision of rural schools, in the interest of the country community.

A New Grouping. One-room school districts should be grouped on a new principle. The county unit is too large and the township is often too small for proper supervision, but the visits of the trained superintendent should be frequent enough to give him intimate command of details in every one of the schools under his charge. This will give some kind of team work in the problem of rural education. The teacher will not be loaded with the whole burden of a separate educational system. Behind him will stand the trained and official supervision of the superintendent; and the country school district will become a part, through his presence and the competition with other neighboring districts which he shall skilfully suggest, of the larger rural community.

Rural School Consolidation. But for most of the schools in the country consolidation and centralization of the schools will be necessary. By this is meant not the assembling of country pupils in the village or town but the organization of the educational problem out among the farms. For the life of a town or village is in an industrial process different from that which controls the life of country people. Farming is the greatest of all vocations, and it needs schools of its own. It is the fundamental and most pervasive of industries, and the schooling of the boy or girl for the farm will be a more effective preparation for all occupations than will the schooling of boys and girls for commerce, for mechanical trades, or for professions.

Districts Merged in One. We believe, therefore, that the schools of the rural community should be merged in one. The country community has a radius of the team haul. The horse-drawn vehicle for a long time to come will standardize the range of rural social experience. At the center, therefore, of the team-haul radius should be built an adequate school building. The one-room schools should be closed. Districts may thus be assembled, two or five or seven or nine in number, and their children transported daily to the central school in wagons hired for that purpose. Nothing will do more for the reorganizing of country life and the cultivation of the community spirit than this daily assembling of the children from the households which have a common experience in the country, to study together the problems of life.

Example of Completed Process. This process has practically been completed in several counties

JOHN SWANEY SCHOOL, PUTNAM COUNTY, ILLINOIS

of northeastern Ohio. They have passed through pioneer, household, and speculative eras, and are in the dawn of organized agriculture. The consolidation of schools is an evidence of their attainment of this maturity.

Modernized Plant and Its Purpose. The consolidated school as it exists in mature communities is a brick building, generally placed on a country road at a point independent of town or village centers. It has four rooms and an auditorium overhead for recreation and for public gatherings. It has in the basement an adequate heating plant with a water-pressure system. The John Swaney school in Putnam County, Illinois, has a room in the basement devoted to manual training. It has in one of the classrooms an apparatus for teaching cooking and sewing, and the auditorium on the third floor is large enough to seat two hundred and fifty people. It is fitted up for basket-ball games. Out-of-doors this school has about twenty-four acres in a beautiful campus shaded with majestic trees and containing a baseball diamond, football gridiron, and several tennis courts. There is also an old school building now turned into a home for the five resident teachers. This school has maintained its teaching courses with a continuous membership year after year. There are four teachers and a principal. Such a school can have—and inevitably it will have—a system of teaching agriculture. For the demand which the farmer is making, either actively or passively of the country school, is that it shall teach scientific agriculture. It will teach not only agriculture but country life, not to make farmers, but to teach children in terms of their own experience. The John Swaney school and the school at Rock Creek have a piece of land devoted to the purposes of an experiment farm. At the John Swaney School this farm supervision is under the Illinois State Experiment Station. This teaching is not for the making of farmers, but men and women. It must be more than a mere school of rural money-making. The teaching of agriculture needed in the schools is for the purpose of training in country life. The country school must make the open country worth while. It will teach agriculture as the basis of an ideal life, rather than as a quick way of profits.

Advantages of Riding to School. Families on the outer bounds of the consolidated school district sometimes complain of its exceptional burdens which fall upon them, but this difficulty inheres in the present system. The small boy who lives on the outer boundary of a school district two miles or three from the one-room school, has exceptional hardships in his daily trudge to school. Many a middle-aged man remembers the chilblains and frosted ears or finger-tips from the long walk to school, and even in summer the weary trudge with books and dinner pail was a burden. In the State of Minnesota, where consolidated schools have been highly perfected, the children who come through the bitter winter in the stages many miles to school arrive in better condition and do better work throughout the day than the children who live near-by and walk.

Results of Religious Motive. These two Illinois schools were consolidated under the influence of religious men. John Swaney is a Quaker and his action in giving land and money for this school was in obedience to the principles of the Quaker Meeting, for the Friends have always been organizers of communities in the country. The group of farmers at Rock Creek, of whom Mr. R. E. Bone was the leader, are Presbyterians and their influence on consolidating the public schools of Rock Creek has been a religious ministry to the community in which their church is the only house of worship. These Christian men have interpreted for their time the duty of Christian citizens in this building up of the community through the schools.

Social and Church Center. The consolidated schools of these mature farming communities in the Middle West are great social centers. The daily coming and going of the children turns the tide of social life toward the center. Dr. Willet M. Hayes of the Department of Agriculture at Washington is an ardent believer in the consolidated school district as the unit in rural life. He believes that at every consolidated school there should be a a church, an experiment farm, a playground, and in one of the public buildings thus provided he would furnish rooms, if necessary, for a rural Young Men's Christian Association. There should be at the center also the residences of the leaders of the community; teachers, preachers, organizers of social life. It would follow, and in these mature communities it does follow, that the streams of social influence would flow in and out of this center and unite the whole countryside. Here the young men and women will form their attachments for a lifetime and here the farmers and their neighbors will meet at the periodic gatherings for recreation. At this center the entertainer, the lecturer and musician, will find their audiences, and hither people will come on the day of rest for their common worship. Inevitably the habits of community fellowship will generate habits of common worship. The community by its own forces thus released and organized will gather around the common center and place there or near at hand the meeting-house for the worship of God.

Sections Organized. Such consolidated schools are numerous in Indiana. There are a few in Pennsylvania. There are several counties organized in northern Iowa. In Georgia a whole section of farming country was settled since the war by people who in slavery days were poor, and their intense social inclinations have led them, on the one hand, to exclude the Negro, and on the other to consolidate their own educational and social interests. Every one of these farming sections has attained to rapid maturity. The centralized country school is at once the effect and the cause of agricultural maturity.

Work of the Agricultural Colleges. Among the strong influences working for the betterment of country life is the extension work of the agricultural colleges. State and national departments of agriculture send out their lecturers, organizers, and demonstrators. These men and women have been in the past ten years the heralds of organized farming. The story of this influence goes back to the Land Grant Act in 1862, by which valuable lands were assigned by the national government to the various States for the purposes of agricultural education. These colleges are therefore at work in every State. For a long time their influence was small. Their teachers were called book farmers. But within the past ten years they have got hold of their work with a more social grasp. This has been accomplished both by the improvement of the courses and by the more thorough scientific training of the teachers, and above all by the extension work of these colleges, through lecturers, demonstrators, and organizers. This is not the place for a canvass of their work. Enough to say that in every State the church or school in the country has a right to claim the services of teachers or lecturers from the State college or State department of agriculture. In some of the States, as in New York, these speakers are furnished within certain limits without cost to the community. These demonstrators are of great value, especially in the South, where they are fighting the battle of the farmer against the enemies of the cotton and the corn crop.

Typical Instances.   A good illustration of their efficiency is in a church in Texas of the Baptist denomination.   The ladies of this church under the guidance of the expert from Washington are regularly hiring a piece of land from a farmer, planting it according to the specifications furnished by the expert, and hiring the tillage of the crop in accordance with his rules.   They have reaped year by year a substantial profit on the transaction for their church funds; but they have done a greater thing in demonstrating to the farmer both that the Church would teach better farming and better living and also that the science of the Washington department is better business.   In Oklahoma there are farmers who under the direction of the Washington expert are leasing land to their tenants and writing into the lease the specifications which require scientific tillage of their soil.   Thus the fertility of the soil is preserved, and the profit both of the farmer and of the owner are raised to the highest point.   There are churches in New York State which, combining to form a farmers' club, invite the experts from Cornell University to lecture year after year in the systematic education of the farmers as to the economic use of their soil and maintenance of it for generations to come.

Value for Church Life.   This use of scientific agriculture is necessary to the upbuilding and to the survival of the country Church.   Professor T. N. Carver, of Harvard University, in a recent address, has insisted that the Church should promote

scientific husbandry in the interest of the whole community and in the interest of its own future. His
thesis is that organized religion in the country is dependent on that intelligence and that economic prosperity which are involved in better farming for its
continued intelligence and for its moral power.

Era of Academies. There was a time when in
country communities there were academies, usually founded by the Churches and owned by them,
which took the place for country people of the college in modern life. They were centers of culture.
Their teachers were classical scholars and they imparted to the sons and daughters of the farmers the
high ideals and the knowledge of the great world
which dignified the household farmer. These
schools had a great influence. They were frankly
religious in their foundation, but with the extension of the high school system under the State control very many of them have been closed. Little
by little the subsidies of Church boards have been
withdrawn, scholars have been unwilling to pay
tuition for this schooling when they could have
good secular training in the high schools in the
near-by towns. This has been a great loss in country life.

May Become Folk Schools. The high school is
cold and indifferent. It is often dominated by
politics and its ideals are generally lower than were
those of the old academy, as the ethical and esthetic
standards are not equal to those of the academy.
It is useless, however, to lament the days which will

never be restored, and the academies are mentioned here in order to suggest that those which can be revived should be transformed into folk high schools, such as have had a great influence in Denmark.[1]

Must Have Country Emphasis. These folk high schools have all the enthusiasm of the modern Chautauqua, with an added thoroughness. They have the precise and orderly curriculum of the old academy, but their term is not more than six months, while the academy course was often as long as six years. Their purpose is industrial training which shall fit the country boy to live in the country and the girl to prefer the farmhouse as her home, while the academies taught a classical culture which introduced the farmer's son into the great world. The suggestion is, therefore, that the academy be completely transformed and the currents of its life reversed. If it is to live in the days to come it shall no longer be a stepping-stone out of the country community, a gangway for going off into the city, but it shall become an anchorage in the country community, an organizing of motives for agriculture and for work.

Ideal Enthusiasm. These folk schools, however, possess one, and it is the central, characteristic of the old academy schools; they are filled with enthusiasm, with a national and patriotic and religious spirit. The old academies were centers of the noblest idealism of their day. They trained men for leadership. The folk schools have been in Den-

[1] See Appendix A.

mark centers of enthusiasm. They have written and sung their own songs. They have filled the whole country with their music and their happy spirit. The following song is one of the most popular in Denmark. It was written by Bishop Grundtvig, the founder of these schools, and this translation is made by Mr. George Koefod Fernström.

Church-bell, lost in great and noisy city,
  Thou wert cast for towns where far and nigh
All can hear whene'er a babe is weeping
  Or a mother sings her lullaby.

When a child I lived near fields and forest,
  Like a heaven to me was Christmas morn,
Like an angel's voice, glad tidings bringing,
  Told thy chimes of joy to mankind borne.

Higher still thy notes my soul uplifted
  When they rang with Easter-sun's first ray,
Chimed: "Rejoice, thy Savior has arisen!
  Thou, too, rise in dawn of Easter-day!"

Lovely, too, in harvest time to hear thee
  In the evening hours with quiet blest,
List'ning, while thy heavenly voice comes floating
  Over earth to call all souls to rest.

Yes, whenever now the curfew tells me
  That the sun is down, the birds asleep,
With the flowers I bow my head and softly
  In between thy strokes this prayer will creep:

Church-bell! tho' my dust shall never hear thee
  Tolling over it, O tell them all,
Cheer my dear ones, tell them thither went he,
  Leaving as the sun sets in the fall.

Use for the Sunday-school. What has been said about common schools rises often to its best in the country in the Sunday-school. The reader asks,

"How shall these things be done?" I would not assert that the Sunday-school can do them all, but the beginning of the reconstruction of a country place is often the founding of a Sunday-school. The limitations of Sunday-school work are well known and you will find these limitations if you do Sunday-school work; but it is well to go ahead to the limit before you try another method. Country people are religious. They believe that their children should learn religion. More than they crave the gospel for themselves, they believe in it for their little ones. It is frequently possible to enlist rough men who know no Scripture and profess no religion in the support of an active school for the children on Sunday, because of the universal belief of all serious men in the necessity of religious training for the young.

Its Appeal to Even Rough Men. There is here a very profound religious thought. The president of a noted theological seminary tells the story of a Sunday-school organizer in Michigan whose work brought him to a godless, disorderly town, with no religious services whatever. When he announced his intention of organizing a Sunday-school the violent element of the community announced that they would break it up. The Sunday-school man went calmly ahead, trusting in God, and his help came from a strange source. Feeling in the community mounted high as Sunday morning approached, and most of the population were present at the meeting to discuss the proposed Sunday-school. When he called for those interested in the school, only a few women responded. But after his address, a rough figure stepped forward from among the men and facing the preacher said that he had " heard tell " that some one was going to break up this Sunday-school. For his part he thought it was bad enough for the grown people in this neighborhood, and he would like to see something done for the children. He concluded his brief remarks by declaring that he could not teach—even within profanely described limits—but he promised to attend the Sunday-school every time it met and stand at the door and " bust " perdition out of any man who tried to interfere. He was the biggest leader of rowdies in the neighborhood and all the rough element feared him. There was really no profanity in his offer: his language was perfectly understood by the crowd, and he was as good as his word. Under his fostering protection, purely physical in outward form, the Sunday-school grew and thrived and shortly had abundance of support from all sources.

A Means of Rural Reconstruction. No other method of religious teaching has so great actual value in America. If the Sunday-school leaders but knew it, they have the vehicle for rural reconstruction. The possibilities of Sunday-school teaching have not been reached, because the leadership of the Sunday-school forces is too often conservative, timorous, and prejudiced. This situation, however, is rapidly changing, for the Sunday-school leadership of the country is taking advanced ground as to the place of the Sunday-school in the solution of all the problems of the Church. The new graded courses are built with the one distinct purpose of training a generation of Christians for faithful and efficient service. This will be a great help, for the essentials for building the rural community are in the Sunday-school, which is interdenominational. It is an elastic and an inexpensive medium of religious work and its appeal is to the young. Above all it is a religious work, and to this day there is no other call which can bring country people to the center of the community all standing at attention to the same degree to which a religious call can assemble them.

Devotional Access to the Community. However, the rule in rural work is to do that for which you have leaders. Bearing in mind, then, that the Sunday-school will be limited in its value by the largeness of mind possessed by its leaders, let us consider it as a means of rural reconstruction. Its first great value is its devotional access to the community. The Sunday-school offers the Bible to country people. It does not need to plead for its cause. They already desire its ministry. It can be therefore the thin edge of the wedge, however broad the head shall be.

Service of the New and Old Testaments. The Sunday-school, therefore, should teach the New Testament for its spirit and the Old Testament for its country life inspiration. The New Testament commands the personal devotion of individuals. It is the great book for leaders. Jesus is the master of the masters of men. The inspiration for individuals who are to serve will be found in his words and in the story of his deeds. In approaching, therefore, the Old Testament as the great book of country life, the scholars should be taken every year into the Gospels and into the story of the early Church for its power of compelling personal devotion.

Authority and Influence of Jesus. The authority of Jesus Christ over the individual soul must always be the clue to every social endeavor. This will be called evangelism by many, and the word is excellent if it be understood in its broadest meaning as a preparation for service. Central to this melting of the heart and offering of it to the community in the name of God must ever be the influence of Jesus himself, in the story of the Gospels for the little children, in the history of his life for adolescents, and in the development of this history through the apostles and the early Church for adults. The influence of this New Testament teaching is overpowering. If the leaders of the community be brought in their preparation directly into contact with the actual story of the Master's life from his birth unto his glorious crucifixion and resurrection, and the tremendous days before he departed from the eyes of men, it will abide with them in all the ministry for which they are being prepared.

Group of Leaders' Study. The value in the Sunday-school of a group study by the leaders themselves must be mentioned. This group is commonly called the teachers' training class, but I shrink from the term because we are considering something more real than such a formal meeting could be. The important thing is to assemble kindred spirits whose devotion can be blended in one. If it be necessary for this purpose to omit any of the teachers, then the group should be assembled in a suitable place, including only those who can be trusted. By all means the center of the community for devotion and for service should be the periodic meeting for the study of the Scripture to be used in the school and for the planning of other work. Here only kindred spirits shall be present who will violate no confidence and who will unite in a devotion to the Master and to the community.

A Meeting for Counsel. Where the uniform lessons are used the weekly lesson will have its place, but this should not be considered formal. The teachers' meeting is not a place for cramming or a substitute for study on the part of the teacher. Where the graded lessons are taught there will be no opportunity for definite lesson study. In either case ample time should be taken up with a study and discussion of methods of teaching. The literature on this subject from a Sunday-school standpoint is abundant, and should be widely used. Anything that will help make a more efficient Sunday-school will be a long step in solving the problem of religious education in the country.

The program should include frank, earnest discussion of every interest of the community and of every person, so far as is helpful, in the community. This meeting should be for the purpose of planning and forwarding the conversion of men and their enlistment in the service of the community. At this place the influence of these leaders should be determined in common and their action toward every project in the whole community should be pledged.

United Prayer and Planning for Community. Such a meeting should never close without devoted and common prayer, not formal, but earnest and shared as far as possible by all. If this central heart of the community cannot beat in terms of prayer, it will not be safe for the openness of speech and frankness of discussion to be observed which I have commended. But if the meeting can be genuinely devotional, then it can be entirely confidential. Such a gathering of leaders central to a working Sunday-school can lift the whole community in the name of Christ.

Gospel of the Country. The Old Testament is the gospel of country life for Christian folk. It is the story of the settlement of a wandering people in a holy land. America is to her people the promised land, but its promise of freedom and of a righteous commonwealth moving in freedom to the ends of justice has not yet been satisfied. We are in America at some such stage of development as is pictured in the Book of Judges. " Every man does what is right in his own eyes," and the great period of the development of the American commonwealth is to come. We are disappointed and disillusioned of many early ideals. Puritanism from New England does not satisfy serious and earnest men as once it did. The Quakerism and the Presbyterianism of Pennsylvania are not convincing to the children of the Quakers and of the Scotch-Irish; nor is the aristocratic faith of the old Southern States believed in the South as once it was believed. Yet the people have hope in God and religious feeling is general throughout the country. Like the Old Testament Jews we are wandering. The farmer is not settled nor contented on the land. When he has secured a competence he does not remain a farmer, but desires to retire to the town. Men are not contented to produce and they do not teach their children to be producers, but more and more the exodus from the country is increasing the class of consumers and diminishing those who raise the food and raw materials. We need the new doctrine which Professor L. H. Bailey of Cornell University describes under the title, "The Holy Earth."

Up-to-date Messages. The teaching of the Old Testament through Sunday-schools is the service which religious people can render in making of the farmer a permanent and a happy tiller of the soil. Its legislation was for an agricultural people and its hymns, which we call psalms, are the songs of a rural people who love the land, the hills and the mountains, as few Americans love the country. Its doctrine of Providence rises to its height in that simplest of the psalms about the shepherd and his sheep. The messages of the prophets were obviously sermons preached by great souls made anxious because the people were deserting the land, and moving into the cities. Isaiah denounces those things which are done to-day in Indiana, Illinois, and Iowa. The evils of absentee landlordism, the decadence of the retired farmer, and the pitiful condition of the tenant farmer are all pictured in the histories and prophecies and the legislation of the Old Testament. It is assuredly not asking too much of the Sunday-school in the country that these lessons of country life should be taught in the same religious spirit in which they were first spoken and written.

Some Required Teachings. Very often the bounds of the Sunday-school are at the covers of the Bible. Few Sunday-school teachers have been able to use the Sunday-school as a means of teaching patriotism, the knowledge of missions, and social service. If the Sunday-school cannot have classes in these great themes, if it is impossible in the country for citizenship so to be taught in a class of men that the buying and selling of votes shall be extinguished by the members of that class in that community, then these classes and groups must be assembled elsewhere. But the Sunday-school is the simplest medium for the teaching of righteousness and of every religious message needed by the community, and in the Sunday-school all these efforts to teach the young and the old in the name of God should be organized.

Call for New Ideals. The great business, however, of the schoolmaster, whether he be paid or unpaid, professional or volunteer, is to idealize country life. Ideals do not come in books, but they grow out of experience. Those which come through books are often imported and artificial. They are cherished in the mind, but not practised in the life. Such ideals are false and delusive. Ideals that are true grow out of situations and conditions. Country life is a great situation, and as " new conditions make new duties," the study of country life rouses men in our day to new services and new work. Therefore the greatest religious ministry which we can render in the country to-day is the dignifying of life and work in the open country. There at our hand are beauty, health, and every spring of sentiment. Mankind loves the country instinctively, if only he may find reasons there for living and sources there of social contentment. The business of the religious leaders is to bring God into the country and make country life a religion. This is what it means to idealize country life. It cannot be imported, but the ideals of country life must be new, modern, and must grow out of the experience of people now living in that country place. Such ennobling of the life of the community will call on every resource of the country Church and of its people. Without this dignifying of the

community there can be no religion for the people
who live there, for they will always be discontented and desiring to live elsewhere. They will
have the heart of nomads and they can never rise
above the morals of nomads, for " Out of the heart
are the issues of life." The business of the country
Church is to convert the heart of the countryman
from the wandering and speculative, discontented
state into the settlement, with happiness and abiding
peace, in the holy land of America.

RURAL MORALITY AND
RECREATION

The "play of the spirit" is not an empty phrase. It is always the spirit that plays. Our bodies only work. The spirit at play is what I mean by the higher life.

Play is the pursuit of ideals. When released from the daily work, the mill we have to tread in order to live, then we strive to become what we would be if we could. When we are free we pursue those ideals which indicate and create character. If they lead us toward wholesome things,—literature, music, art, debate, golf, tennis, horseback riding, and all of the other things that are wholesome and good,— then our lives are rounded out, balanced, and significant.

If education is "equipping for life," then it ought to be divided into two parts, equipment for work and equipment for play. If education is bound to provide us with the luxuries of the body, it ought also at least to furnish us with the necessities of the soul. It must tell us, not only how to get the most out of the working hours, but also how to spend most profitably and joyously the hours that remain.—*Luther H. Gulick*

The Church must provide directly or indirectly some modern equivalent for the huskings, apple bees, quiltings, and singing schools of the old days. In some way or other young men and young women must have opportunity for unconstrained intercourse, free from self-consciousness and artificiality. This may take the form of clubs, parties, picnics, excursions, or what you please. One rule is absolute: the Church must not attempt to take away the theater, the dance, the card party, unless it can give in its place, not merely a religious or intellectual substitute, like a prayer-meeting or a literary society, but a genuine social equivalent.—*William DeWitt Hyde.*

Our argument rests upon the favorable showing of the country as a whole as compared with the city as a whole. As tested by the symptoms of degeneracy, the country is in as healthful a state as the city, where the advantages and wholesome influences of civilization are massed; where education is at its best; where eloquence finds its opportunity, and art gathers its treasures; where wealth commands all resources, and taste has every gratification; where churches are powerful, and every social institution coöperates in the exaltation of human life. That the country is not distanced by the city in social and moral development almost exceeds belief, or to use the terms with which we began, the line of averages in social and moral values is at a surprising height in the country. Now if a part of the rural communities fall below this line, then other communities rise above it; assuredly as many are above as below the line, or it is falsely called an average.—*Wilbert L. Anderson*

IV

RURAL MORALITY AND RECREATION

New Estimate of Play. Religious people have always recognized the close connection between the amusements of the community and public morals. The churches of old times used to forbid their members to attend meetings for amusement. The ethical character of play was recognized, but the austere policies of the Church recognized only its immoral tendencies. In modern times serious people look on play as a moral process, having close and intimate relations with conscience. What we do for hire, or under the orders of other people, or in the routine of life is done because we have to. We do not choose the minor acts of study in school, of work in the factory, of labor on the house, of composition in writing a book. All these little acts are part of a routine which is imposed upon us and we call them work. But play is entirely voluntary. Every action is chosen, and expresses will and preference. Therefore, play is highly moral. It is the bursting up of our own individuality, and it expresses, especially in the lesser things, the preferences of life.

Moral Value of Team-work. Especially is teamwork, which characterizes organized play, influen-

tial in training men in the minor moralities. I am
going to plead in this chapter for these little moralities, the lesser goodnesses of life. The great
school for training men in these little things
that make up the bulk of character is team-
work and coöperation in play. Here is the school
of obedience to others, of self-sacrifice for a company and for a common end, of honor and truthful-
ness, of the subordination of one to another, of
courage, of persistent devotion to a purpose, and of
coöperation. "The reason why farmers cannot co-
operate when they are grown up," says a well-
known country minister, "is in the fact that they
did not learn team-play when they were boys.
They never learned to work together and they cannot obey one another."

Religious Basis of Morals. There are some
Christian people who do not care to train men in
morality. I sat in a public religious assembly during a tedious discussion over a temperance report.
The advocates of temperance desired ample time
for their subject, and finally secured it. At one moment in the discussion a black-clad clergyman leaned
back impatiently in his seat and said, "What is the
use of all this bother? It is nothing but a moral
question, anyway!" Such a man will have no
sympathy with the demand for ethical training.
But the sources of morality are in religious faith.
The great imperatives of personal duty are locked
up with the belief in God and the devotion of the
soul to Jesus Christ. My purpose in this chapter

is to urge that recreation be used by religious people as a means of moral discipline and for the training of young people and working people in righteous character, both in little and in great things.

Country Temperance Work. The first word on this subject must be to the praise of the country Church in its work for the temperance movement. Thirty years ago temperance meant pledge-signing. It was not then a rural movement as to-day it is. The whole scope of temperance reform in those days consisted in securing individual pledges. Men were enlisted as total abstainers and the bulk of the movement was measured by the number who had signed the pledge. Not only drunkards and tipplers were solicited, but the lists were filled with the names of boys and girls and of sober, serious people. It was like a great many other individualist movements.

Growth of Local Option. The service of the country Church has been to socialize the temperance movement. The farmer has learned to hate the saloon. Under the leadership of country churches, which became the centers of discussion, temperance reform has been made a community reform. It has been transferred from pledge-signing to local option. In some States it has become a commonwealth reform. In these instances the State is predominantly agricultural, and the farmers vote for State-wide prohibition. But the most general and the most mighty temperance reform in America has been the farmer's movement for local option. The pledge has been signed by communities and by counties. This has been wrought within the past twenty years. No one can say that the country Church is decadent or without force while this splendid record attests its virility and its social power. The temperance movement, however, is cited at this point as an illustration of the moral duty of country churches in building communities. The temperance reform is only half completed. It has been a negative movement for the expulsion of saloons from communities. The country community is empty, swept, and garnished, but in this process no positive or constructive moral work has been done. There is need of deliberate upbuilding of country life by the country Church.

Constructive Work Needed. This weakness of temperance reform is illustrated in a town in New England from which the sale of liquor has been abolished for a quarter of a century. Moreover, the law is generally observed. There is no fault to be found with the temperance principles of this town, but temperance people and temperance reforms have no influence there. There is neither a local option nor a prohibition list of voters. It is impossible to arouse any interest in temperance, because the policies of the temperance movement have been so purely negative. Their success has been self-effacing. No sooner are they enacted and observed than their influence is erased. This town, however, is far from being a good town. The standards are low. The one church in the town is weak,

though the people are religious. There are about
forty votes for sale in every election and these
voters who are for sale determine the character of
the town. Leading citizens condone the sale of
votes as a necessary evil. Moreover, there is a
certain number of young men and women in the
town who are immoral. Year by year the presence
of this fixed measure of immorality testifies to the
existence of causes of wrong-doing. There is no
organization of the town for moral training.
Among certain people low standards prevail and
nobody is attempting to raise their standards. It
was not enough, therefore, for the moral betterment of this town, to expel the saloon. There must
be brought in something as powerful for good as
the saloon was for evil. It is within the power of
the country Church to organize the people for well-
doing just as much as it was in her power to organize them against ill-doing.

Enlistment of Recreation. The organizations to
accomplish this end will be recreative. Not that
these are the only constructive moral methods.
Universal education has done a great service for
public morality. One does not need to write books
now urging the Church to support the common
schools. I will not be understood, therefore, as
urging anything except that which can now be effi-
ciently added by the Church to the moral culture
of the people. The business of the Church is to
promote that which being added can accomplish the
greatest good.

Its Moral Worth Demonstrated. The experience of recent years has shown that organized play has moral, constructive power. The Young Men's Christian Association and similar bodies have used gymnasiums and playgrounds for the development of physical life, and have discovered that unwittingly ethical service has been done to those whose bodies they thought to improve. At first Associations put the entrance to the gymnasium near the entrance to the prayer-meeting, believing that the prayer-meeting alone could justify the gymnasium. Now they see that the gymnasium has values of its own, and the best of these values are the moral gains attained by those who take part in the organized play of the Association.

Young Women's Christian Association. The Young Women's Christian Association has with even finer appreciation used recreation for the building of character. They have discovered in open-air games, and in the associations of club life for girls, in the gymnasium and in that greatest essential of all, the constant friendly association of young persons, that moral character is strengthened and the individual is sustained by standards arising from intercourse, from spontaneous action, and from fellowship.

Recent Extension of Play. Settlement workers too have experimented in the play exercises among the children of the poor. Most of these workers are sons and daughters of the churches. They enter their service in a religious spirit. They have come to believe that play has power to build up conscience and character. Of course this building up is in the littles of small brick and mortar, but the best constructions in character are made of the infinitely small. The worst undermining of character is in the details of daily conduct. Dr. Luther H. Gulick is perhaps the highest authority among religious and educational and humanitarian people upon this subject, and he teaches that play, because of its highly voluntary character, trains men in a better morality than does work.

Pioneer Era Without Play. The story of play and of morality is interwoven with the development of life in the open country. In the pioneer period of American farming morality showed the vices and virtues of independence. Pioneers are lonely people and they have no social virtues. They should not be expected to have them. Men cannot live through the days of a year alone, and then practise when called on the virtues of close social life. The churches of the pioneer period inculcate the virtues of independence. The great transaction is to them the salvation of the individual soul, and they teach that other moral processes are probably sinful. Amusements in this period were few. Among the mountaineers in the South to-day there is no play. Even the children are solitary. Teamwork outside of the town is unknown. They who attend meetings for amusement are rebuked for it. The recreations of pioneers and mountaineers are deeds not of team-work, but of personal prowess.

The great men of the time before Lincoln did deeds of prowess with the gun and the ax. They wrestled, they ran, but they did not play in any organized form.

Pioneer Sins and Vices. The pioneer period, as it was individualist, showed the vices of an unorganized society. Acts of men were condemned by the early churches which were impulsive rather than deliberate. Many were the adulteries, thefts, and breaches of contract of those days, but in the most of cases they expressed independence of spirit. The sins of later times expressed a coöperation in wrong-doing. The religious worker among pioneer or mountain people must deal with them in sympathy. He must recognize the splendid independence of character of which they are capable and teach them the nobility of the solitary life of the mountain.

Only Safe Method of Change. In pioneer churches, also, the moral problem is very largely one of adaptation. The largest section of pioneer life is in the Southern mountains and on the Western frontier. But the pioneer period is yielding to the invasion of modern industry. In all these places the Church must help the people to enter the new era. This can be done best through the young. But the fundamental method of teaching it must be economic. The great struggle of a people to whom the railroad has come and who are solicited to work in mills is to get a living. For instance, in Huntsville, Alabama, are some thousands of moun-

taineers who have been brought to the city to work
in the cotton mills. They are country people, living in " company houses." Out of the loneliness of
mountain cabins they come to be crowded into congested, slumlike villages. Observers testify that
the general tendency of factory labor upon these
mountain people is good on one condition; namely,
that they have religious leadership in the transition
from the mountain to the city. If they have settlement workers going among them to help those who
fall, if there be a friendly visitor or district nurse
at hand to care for the sick or for those who are
injured in the mill, then the new industrial period
will be a blessing. The mill itself, with its better
wages and its steady employment, is one vast school
for the mountaineer, but without the blessing of
religious and voluntary Christian service among
them, the mountain people will get no benefit. This
is the testimony of mill owners, settlement workers,
philanthropists, and Christian ministers.

Twofold Christian Work. The service, therefore,
which Christian people can render is both in maintaining the pioneer type of men and of community,
and in helping these communities to enter into the
organized life which comes upon them with railroads, factories, and organized farming.

Household Moral Standard. The household
period of farming has its moral system grouped
around the household unit. As the individual was
the unit in the farmer period with independence
of character as the clue to all virtues, so here the

household is the unit. The virtues of the working household, earning its living from its own soil, are the virtues of this time. There was no play in the pioneer period, but the beginnings of recreative life came with the warmer and more social, neighborly intercourse of household farming. The austere ideas of this period, however, treated recreative enterprises with severity. The early churches forbade their members " to go to frolics." The surest way to signify that play was moral was to declare it immoral and to forbid it. President Henry C. King says that many parents express their brief philosophy of childhood in one word, " Don't." In the same way the austerity of this time troubled itself but little with the discovery of possible good, and too easily condemned all spontaneous recreative enterprises by calling them evil and forbidding them.

Narrow Outlook. The household farmer is so devoted to his own group and its experiences that he approves of what is within and disapproves of most things without. He looks upon all other groups of people with a certain reserve, almost an aversion. He favors the members of his own household and prefers them to all others. The curve of his approval and appreciation falls very rapidly at the outer boundaries of his home and his farm. He does not recognize obligations in extensive detail outside of his own farm. He thinks of his neighbor farmers as his competitors, not his comrades in a coöperative enterprise. But the household farmer has not matured his system of tilling the land sufficiently to appreciate that his success is dependent on his neighbor's success. This competitive and divisive condition of farming is the source of many moral conditions in the country which are evil. It is the source, too, of much of the waste of country life.

Strange Moral Bias. The prevalence of this competitive state of mind in the country and its profound influences are amazing. One sees men who are pillars of the churches working for their own families and giving nothing for the interests of the community. It is a shocking moral experience to observe deacons and other spiritual leaders of country communities using the public school system for private profit and thinking no ill of it. They have no sense of the community, because they have never coöperated in the essentials with their neighbors. Therefore, they see no wrong in using the public school as a source of income for a member of their family. They would not tamper with school funds, but they will solicit the appointment of a daughter as a teacher solely because she is a member of their family. There are many farmers in the country who could be trusted with your property or with your child. You would make no mistake if you appointed such a man executor of your will, but beware of putting him as the trustee of a public fund which is for the interest of the community. These men have a sense of family life, but as to public trust, they have it not.

Religious Inconsistency. The evil to be cured

is the evil which expresses itself in packing the good apples at the top and the poor ones in the middle of the barrel. It is the evil of refusal to recognize social standards, on which alone cities can be built, by which alone the world market can be organized. In a church in New York State is a prominent and excellent citizen, approved by his neighbors. The milk from his dairy farm by which he gets his living was refused by the health officers of the city of Rochester, and he was informed of the reasons for the disapproval. His standards of social conduct were so low that instead of improving the sanitary quality of his milk, he turned his back on Rochester and, driving in the opposite direction, sent his milk to Buffalo, where he could sell it at a little more pains and at somewhat less profit. This religious man, uninstructed in the social standards by which a countryman serves unseen customers in a great city, then boasted of his evading the sanitary restrictions of Rochester.

Indifference to Results Out of Sight. A pastor found a boarding-place in the country for a mother with a very sick child. The farmer when he saw the pitiful condition of the little baby promptly offered his sympathetic help to the mother in restoring it to health. Believing, as other farmers did, that the milk produced by cattle fed on green corn is bad for little children, he offered to set aside one cow from his herd and feed that cow on grass alone, because the herd at that time was feeding on green corn. The little child very promptly recovered abundant health. Yet all the time this farmer was sending his milk produced by the cows fed on green corn to the city for sale, while knowing that it would be used by children and believing that children so nourished would grow sick and die. The child seen impressed his mind, but the children unseen had no influence upon his conduct. The need in this case is of cultivation in social standards. Household farming produced no community standards of action.

Need of Frequent Happy Meetings. Sometimes the people of a given neighborhood have no experience of a common interest which unites a whole community. Probably for most of them the moral standards of organized and scientific farming will never come. One cannot always hope to teach grown people the lessons which they did not learn as children. The business of the Church, therefore, is to organize the young children, and train them in the reactions and instinctive responses of a new mode of life. This can be done by all forms of recreative and social life, especially if they are organized for a high purpose. Professor Carver has rightly insisted that recreative life in the country does not need to be musical or dramatic or gymnastic, or any other one prescribed thing, but the essential is that it result in frequent and happy social meetings.

Trials of Transition. It must be remembered that the Church has not the whole task. Every agency of modern life is coöperating to undermine the standards of the household era, or rather to enlarge them, through a period of speculation, to the standards of organized and scientific agriculture. The Christian worker who is earnest for the enlargement of the mind of country people must recognize through what bitter experiences the farm household has gone, when so many farmers have sold the land on which their ancestors were buried; how mighty the emotional change has been in the past twenty years when men have given up the homesteads for which their fathers and grandfathers labored and even fought, and in which the whole round of their life has been passed.

Reconstructive Opportunity. "A period of reconstruction is a religious opportunity," says one of our great missionaries. This profound social experience of change makes possible the teaching of new moral standards in the country. The dissolution of the household group leaves individuals separated, confused, often depressed by the new period, and unable to act by the old standards; unable to learn what are the new. I am confident that the business of the Church at this time is not only to preach new moral standards, but to organize the people on the principles of the new economy. Indeed, this process of organizing country people is going on. The coöperative spirit is abroad and is doing its work. The need is that the churches should have a part of this spirit, and give the sanction of religious authority, persuasion, and interpretation to the new time. The minister should speak

MAKING A COMMUNITY PARK

SCHOOLS WERE CLOSED AND EVERYBODY TURNED OUT TO HELP

with a sure voice and the people in the country
should enter heartily into every coöperative enterprise that will build up the country community.
This ought to be done confessedly and frankly in
the name of Christ. The religious spirit must be
poured into the new unions of country people. It
will guide them to better efficiency and it will
lift them from the baser and more material ends
to which they will naturally gravitate.

Place for New Ideals. Christianity makes ideals,
and country life at this time needs the ideals of a
new era. The leaven of Christianity has power to
idealize, to dramatize life, and the churches should
train men in the part which they are to play in the
period of organized and scientific farming.

Farm Trafficking in the Middle West. Speculative agriculture characterizes the present day. We
are in the midst of a period of exploiting farm land.
Cash and money values seem to be the curse of
country life. Eastern farmers are amazed at the
selling and reselling and selling again of the farms
in the Middle West. There is far more tenacity
of ownership still in the East, where some farms
are permanently abandoned, than in the Middle
West, where every acre is eagerly sought; for this
speculative selling and buying has had but little
check there, and the community has greatly suffered.

Moral Gains even of Farm Speculation. But the
period of exploiting the farm has its own moral
standards. Country life has not known the values
of cash, and country people have been slow to learn

the obligations which are expressed in terms of money. Farmers who had agreed to sell at a certain figure have too often broken their word when they thought a better price could be obtained by so doing. Few farming communities show the high principle in matters of money which characterizes the Wall Street broker and the banker, whose standards in other things are by farmers much condemned. The banker and the broker know the obligations of money. They live in the terms of cash, and they keep their word. The virtues of a speculative period are virtues which the farmer needs to learn. This period is not mere destruction to the community. It is described by Professor Ross as "the period of redistribution of land values." Professor Carver says, "The American farm lands are passing into the hands of those who will till them to the best advantage." There are rights and wrongs even in a speculative period.

Virile Teaching on Giving. How shall the Church raise the standard of morality in a time of speculation? The great business of the Church in this time is to exalt the doctrine of consecration of money. Like other moral standards it comes more by experience than by precept. Sermons and teachings will affect it, but the doing of deeds by people themselves means more than sermons spoken to them or lessons drawn for them by word of mouth. The country Church should teach its people to give. The organization of the work of the Church on a basis of giving will have a profound and far-reach-

ing influence. " Pay to the Lord what you owe "
is a gospel needed in the country community. This
doctrine must be taught in a virile and not in a
merely persuasive manner. The Church must be
supported, not by the condescending benevolence
of a few, but by the consecrated dues of the many.

Recreations Worth their Cost. The Church
among working people, who have little money, must
solve the questions of paid entertainments. Recreations should not be paid for out of the collection
plate. People are willing to pay for them. Their
value in assembling the whole community is very
great.

Three Principles. I suggest therefore three principles by which they be governed. First, entertainments should pay for themselves. All clubs or
societies in a church should pay as they go. Second, they should not be used as a source of income
for the church. Worship must not exploit recreation. The minister must not get his salary from
oyster suppers or private theatricals, for if these
things are used for church support they will become
baser and poorer in quality. Third, paid entertainments should be in another room than that used
for worship, if it is possible. These three principles
may be condensed into one: that worship and
recreation are separate enterprises of the Church.
Each must be managed in its own times, and for
its own values.

Frank, Definite Action. There can be no building up of moral character in the country till minis-

ters and church people are earnest and businesslike.
There must be frank, definite, virile action. Its
basis must be clear-cut and its administration resolute. The Church which has positive ideas as to
the Lord's ownership and the sacredness of all
money obligations will do much to build up the
country community, and it will be found that this
Church has built the moral character of its people.

Church Social Leadership Desirable. The highest moral values will not be attained unless this
social opportunity be given by the Church. It is
of the greatest ethical importance that religion be
the center of the moral life. There is no other organizing power so strong and no other has such
immediate appeal. Whatever city people may do,
country folk expect the Church to train the conscience. The mere gathering of people at a church
tends to remind them of every moral principle and
to awaken every ennobling association. The standards of Christianity are the highest moral standards,
so that it is all-important that the Church be the
leader in the moral culture of the community. In
our day it is most generally to be done by definite
organizations for building up the social life of the
country.

Summary. To sum up this chapter, then, the
problem of morality is intimately related in the
country community with the play experience of the
people. The one reflects the form of the other.
Amusements in the country are often immoral.
Recreation may be made in the highest degree a

moral power. The organized industries all react upon their workers in a craving for organized play. This play is the voluntary expression of those whose work is in little details involuntary. Therefore, play is highly moral. It is the expression of the spontaneous, voluntary, personal impulses. The pioneer period had the vices of an independent people. Those who would train solitary farming people must at once respect their independent character: transform them so far as is possible by the infusion of social spirit; but all the time the solitary and independent character must be treated in its own terms. Household farming should produce family virtues, yet the virtues of the household period of farming are disappearing before the era of speculative and scientific farming, to which these virtues are inadequate. The children of the household farming era need to be trained in the organized and coöperative virtues of more mature agriculture. Country people need to be trained in the giving of money. The ethical standards of a financial life need cultivation among country people, because at the present time we are in the period of speculative farming, when values are expressed in money and obligations are those in which the Christian banker is the ideal type. Last of all, the virtues of coöperation are the highest, and the vices of competition are the worst, which at the present time we must recognize. The great business of the religious and moral leader in the country is to train men in coöperative life.

COÖPERATION AND FEDERATION

The Country Life movement deals with what is probably the most important problem before the English-speaking peoples at this time. Now the predominance of the towns, which is depressing the country, is based partly on a fuller application of modern physical science, partly on superior business organization, partly on facilities for occupation and amusement; and if the balance is to be redressed, the country must be improved in all three ways. There must be better farming, better business, and better living. These three are equally necessary, but better business must come first. For farmers, the way to better living is coöperation, and what coöperation means is the chief thing the American farmer has to learn.—*Horace Plunkett*

Very much has been said about the necessity of business coöperation among farmers, and the importance of the subject can hardly be overstated; and yet it should be understood that economic coöperation is only one of many means that may be put in operation to propel country life. The essential thing is that country life be organized: if the organization is coöperative, the results—at least theoretically—should be the best; but in one place, the most needed coöperation may be social, in another place educational, in another religious, in another political, in another sanitary, in another economic in respect to buying and selling and making loans or providing insurance. When the chief deficiency in any region is economic, then it should be met by an organization that is primarily economic.—*L. H. Bailey*

In the little town of Victor, Montana, Presbyterians, Baptists, and Methodists have not progressed quite far enough in Christian unity to feel that they can belong to one church, but they are far enough along to live and work as one church. So they have taken one of their local houses of worship for preaching services and the other for Sunday-school. They have Presbyterian preaching two Sundays in the month, and Baptist and Methodist preaching one Sunday each. But their Sabbath-school and their Christian Endeavor Society run on week after week as united bodies, without denominational distinctions. A Sunday-school of 150 they find a great deal more spirited and a great deal more effective than would be three Sunday-schools of fifty each. And the same consideration in their opinion amply justifies the joint young people's work. This victory of Victor over denominational rivalries should be more than suggestive—it should be strongly incitative—to other over-churched villages.—*The Continent*

V

COÖPERATION AND FEDERATION

Occasional United Effort. Coöperation may be
occasional among people who are indisposed to it,
or it may be social among those who are accustomed, with reserve, to act together, or it may be
fundamental and continuous among country people
who depend upon it for their livelihood. Solitary
farming was uncoöperative. Only occasional acts
in emergencies were coöperative. Pioneer and
settler folk did not enlist in armies, except under
terrifying emergencies. They did not gather for
common work, except as the exigencies of pioneer
life required them, for a barn-building or a house-
raising. They had no settled or regulated or required coöperation. Yet there was in this period
at times a more fundamental coöperation, because
it was an effort to secure necessities of life. The
life of pioneer days is centrifugal. It goes off into
the wilderness and retreats toward the center only
when driven in.

Unfederated Religious Stage. The religious life
of solitary farmers was equally innocent of federation. They believed with all their hearts in division.
The people of this type in the country to-day believe

that the virtuous state is that in which the few righteous are separate from the many. To them the activities of the church which represents the whole community are presumably worldly. Social unity means worldliness, but the separation of a small group gives them a consciousness of piety.

Strong Stress on the Individual. This unco-operative religious life idealizes the individual. God is known to be a person, but they think that he is not served in a society. How different is this ideal from the modern growing conception of the community devoted to God! How unlike is the pioneer ideal of solitary living, imposed upon them by the wilderness and the prairie, to the present social conception of the service to God in the service to a community or to a society!

Extreme Individual Views. This doctrine of religious individualism can be carried to terrifying and tragic ends. There have been lonely Elijahs in America who believed that they alone were left of all God's prophets. I am not concerned in this chapter to note the moral values of this independence. These moral values are very great. But in the present time the independent and solitary conception of God is too often a source of weakness in the community and of unreligion in the Church.

Coöperation for Social Ends. In the period of household farming coöperation in the getting of a livelihood was only occasional. Household farming still prevails over most of the United States, unsettled and weakened by speculation as it is, and coöperation among household farmers is purely social. It is not economic. They visit, they dine, they go to common places of meeting, they inter-marry. The social processes of the country are co-operative, but the weakness of purely social co-operation is shown in the inability of household farmers to resist the speculative process that is now undermining the social economy of the household farmer.

Economic Coöperation also Essential. Only those farmers are able to resist the dissolving acid of speculation who coöperate economically. Those farmers are, speaking broadly, in three classes. The first class is illustrated in the Mormons in the West, who coöperate in getting their livelihood under the organizing power of their churches. Secondly, the Scotch and Scotch-Irish Presbyterians, who co-operate in the building of their communities, and in a larger measure in their economic life, than other farmers do, and third, the Pennsylvania Germans, a name which is applied to a group of re-ligious bodies who coöperate in their social and their economic life. With them belong other Teutonic populations living in the open country. The suc-cess of these farmers in resisting the process of speculation, in holding their land, in keeping up their communities and maintaining their country churches, is due to the fact that they make com-mon interest of getting a living. They stand by one another in economic efforts. This thoroughness of coöperation is, according to Sir Horace Plunkett, essential to the welfare of rural life. In his book,[1] Sir Horace insists that merely religious or social organization is not sufficient in the country, but coöperation must be economic, if it is to maintain communities and build up a permanent population. The close dependence of religious institutions upon economic processes is shown by the survival of the churches among those farmers who coöperate in their business, and the weakening of the churches among those farmers who do not. The economic experience of the people is matched in their religious experience. For every economic process one may expect to find a religious effect. For this reason the farmers of the household type of farming, who coöperate only in the genial and pleasant and kindly things of life, but who compete in the serious and stern task of getting a living, have done nothing to resist the process of speculation, and their churches have been undermined by the dissolution of their communities.

Example of Oberlin. The historic experience of John Frederic Oberlin in Waldersbach is an illustration of this thorough coöperation of the whole community. Oberlin came to these people when their community in the mountains of the Vosges was poor, distracted, and discouraged. His predecessors had preached and taught in the schools, but Oberlin saw that he must build up the community from the bottom. He began, therefore, by summoning his neighbors to the task of road building.

[1] *The Rural Life Problem in the United States.*

JOHN FREDERIC OBERLIN

Against their amazed protest he laid the stones with his own hands and demonstrated that as a student of engineering he could serve their common needs. He promoted better agriculture. He undertook the general economic welfare of the community as a whole. His life [1] is a classic in the literature of the country Church.

Requires Care of the Poor. One of the most essential forms of economic coöperation among country people is the care of the poor in the country community. It is a part of the coöperation in getting a living which tends to build the community and to steady the country Church. Where the poor have been neglected and the stupid have been ignored the community has given its energies forth in the lives of the brilliant and the rich and saintly people. There the country Church has been misdirected, and the community has been dissolved, because the poor have degenerated and the stupid have become more ignorant. People of commonplace religious character have retrograded and have remained in the locality, but the brilliant and the rich and the saintly have very generally gone off, leaving the community bereft of leaders and sinking in its own degenerate leavings.

Pennsylvania German Coöperation. The Pennsylvania Germans have built many communities. They have not practised in their permanent communities the intensity and the violence of coöperative life which distinguished them in the cloister of

---

[1] A. F. Beard, *The Story of John Frederic Oberlin.*

Ephrata. In this university about 1730 they initiated an experiment in coöperation and for nearly thirty years under the leadership of Conrad Beissel they blended all the interests of a group of people in one intense glorious effort at communism. This effort failed, and the community reverted from its intense unity to the ordinary free coöperation which prevails among the Mennonite, Dunker, Amish, and other kindred sects. But the history of Ephrata has remained the precious tradition both of their children and of the Pennsylvania people generally and of all readers of American history. Its central principle was religious. It illustrates this fact: that religious life idealizes the labor of poor people for a living; that country people and working people may find in the religious passion the power which will unite them for economic coöperation, and if that coöperation be not so intense or so passionate, the fervor and the enthusiasm necessary will be supplied by religious experience. The Pennsylvania Germans who supply the market around many Pennsylvania towns coöperate to-day quite effectively, though more freely, in their agriculture.

Church Registers Measure of Coöperation. The measure of the coöperative spirit in any population is expressed in the churches. The life of the pioneers showed itself in their many churches. They believed in independent religious organizations. We idealize federation. They built in competition. The churches of the household period were divided, because the household farmer perfects his own family group, but cherishes no community ideal. His churches, therefore, represent the common religious interest of a group of households. The household farmer does not desire to serve the community religiously. He insists that the first duty of the Sunday-school is to teach the children of the families of the church. He is willing that others should attend, but he does not solicit their presence in his church. The leading officer of such a church in central Illinois, when his minister proposed to evangelize the surrounding countryside, said, pointing to the church spire, "That bell can be heard for ten miles. If they want to come to our church, they know when the church is open."

Competition Means Many Churches. With amazing precision the Church is faithful to the economic experience of the people. If the people are uncoöperative in getting their livelihood, the churches are competitive, no matter how kindly the neighbors may be to one another. If their work life is divided, their churches are many.

Speculation Disintegrates. The speculative period of farming tends to dissolve all existing units. Speculation is a valuing of all things in cash, and cash is a personal possession. The more money a man has, the more he is drawn apart from his relatives, from his neighbors, and from his friends. When a man becomes very rich he must always question whether he has any friends, and he is continually annoyed because he has relatives. Wealth capitalizes personality. Private property is the clothing of individualism. The result is that the period of exploitation has dissolved the rural household, undermined the country Church, and caused the country community to disintegrate. Its effect upon rural society is revolutionary.

Strength of Coöperative Elements. I have indicated above that this speculative process is retarded in those farming populations where economic coöperation prevails. The families of the Pennsylvania German hold together, and they are buying the farms which their neighbors abandon. There is no price on their own acres, and they make all sacrifices to better themselves through the speculation in farming from which their neighbors are suffering. Mormons, because of their economic coöperation, are powerful farming people. They extend themselves by their mass activity. In both these cases the churches in which the people worship are maintained and their religious life has continuous power, because they are able to resist the speculative processes which affect their neighbors. They do not find it necessary to federate their churches in the interest of survival, because they have an anchorage in the economic unity of their people. Their churches are all the stronger in the hold upon the individual, because they are the societies by which the business life of the people is compacted. To use a metaphor, the Pennsylvania German's church is his labor union.

Means for Community Institutions. The federa-

tion of churches has a resource, during the speculative period of farming, in the cash which has come
into the country. The farmer has been poor. The
period immediately after the Civil War withered
and impoverished everything connected with the
farm. In that period no proposals could be made
for the betterment of the community because all
common interests were lacking in resources. Such
prosperity as farmers enjoyed enabled them sepa-
rately to survive, but now the time has come when
the farmer through speculation and exploitation has
sufficient means for building community institutions.

A Few Can Benefit Many. This principle works
both ways. Not only are there people in the community who have money, but speculation has impoverished very many. It follows that community
building means the creation of institutions in which
the money of the few shall minister to the need
of the many. In this I have no reference to pauperism. I am thinking only of the needs of working and substantial people who have no capital and
no land.

Union Through Large Gifts. The country community may be united through the gifts of the
prosperous. In many New England towns the old
church is endowed. A few people have prospered
and through their benefactions the many are united
in worship or in service. In the old church at Unity,
Pennsylvania, the gifts of well-to-do people have
been a primary factor in uniting the whole commun-

ity. The brilliant minister and the doctrine of unity he teaches have made use of these gifts, but the prosperity of the few has made the community possible for the many. An essential factor in federating the churches will be the large gifts of those who believe in the community.

May Solve Problem of Church Consolidation. These gifts are only possible in a time of speculative profits, so that the federation of churches now needed in the country community can be greatly helped by the gifts of those who have exploited the resources of the country. A country church in New York State, in which many denominations were represented, was made possible by the munificence of one man, whose money was made by borrowing from his farmer neighbors at four per cent. and loaning to the railroads at ten per cent. He insisted that the church sustained by his money be undenominational. Such a church alone could have survived in that community. The outcome illustrated the value of a large financial gift in settling the intricate problems of church federation.

A Step Toward Church Federation. The federation of churches will in most places await the growth of the coöperative spirit among the farmers. It is impossible for people who are divided in their economic life to be united in their religious life. The spirit of competition in business will breed a competitive religious spirit. Those who are daily contending will not on the day of worship unite. It is a hopeful sign of Church federation that the

GRANGE HALL

"THE GRANGE UNITES MEN INSTEAD OF DIVIDING THEM"

spirit of coöperation is extending among country people. As soon as farmers have recognized that they can work together, they will themselves apply the same principle to their churches.

Unifying Effect of the Grange. This federating influence is exerted by the Grange. This order, which is nominally secret, but really an open fraternal order of country people, is so unlike a lodge that it is generally not found in those communities in which lodges are numerous. The Grange unites men instead of dividing them. Like other orders it has its weaknesses and tends to fall into disrepair, but at its best the Grange has a unifying power in the country community. Especially in the community in which religious people cannot come to agreement in religious matters the Grange infuses a spirit of union among them, through the discussion of everyday interests and the fine social pleasures which it furnishes.

Not Thoroughgoing Enough. The great weakness of the Grange is its lack of economic coöperation. No farmers' organization which has not the courage and thoroughness to get under the farmer's income and bring about coöperation in the securing of a livelihood is adequate to the present situation. The Grange has attempted coöperation in buying. It has in certain places united the farmers in co-operative creameries and other such enterprises, but these have generally been abandoned and the function of the Grange has been limited to that of social coöperation. This is the great weakness of

an order otherwise so extensive and so influential.
The faults of the Grange are those that arise from
this superficial attack upon the problems of rural
life. It is in danger always of becoming a mere
social and pleasure-providing organization and of
omitting more serious aims.

Good Educative Influence. Nevertheless the general influence of the Grange is to accustom country
people to working together. It enables them to
meet, to discuss given interests, and to get used to
the experiences of coöperative effort. They learn
to obey and to command, to serve in appointed and
delegated places, and to depend upon one another,
to keep appointments, and to meet problems as they
arise which affect the community, to devote themselves to interests larger than their own homes or
their own properties.

Successful Examples a Help. There is great hope
also for the union of farmers in their economic and
their religious life in the coöperative experiences of
other sections of the country. Farmers in Dela-
ware and Maryland who have restored the old depleted lands on the Eastern Shore by small fruit
culture are coöperating both in buying and selling
through their produce exchanges. The experience
of these farmers has uncovered certain principles
heretofore unknown. Contrary to all expectation
they have found it profitable to raise throughout
a district the same crop, finding that a better market
is secured for a carload of uniform berries than
for a carload made up of different varieties

and competing consignments of fruit. Such coöperation when once established has power to continue. It is a restraint in times of prosperity and it is a resource in times of depression. Above all, it accustoms country people to coöperate through their constant experience of working together, of sacrificing for one another, and of securing larger gains through these experiences. When one thinks that until these modern experiences of coöperation there have been in America no foci of coöperative life among country people, one is not surprised at the divided condition of churches and the competitive religious life of the country.

Pacific Coast Fruit Growers. The fruit growers of the Pacific Coast have been obliged to coöperate in order to sell their product. Shipping as they do across a whole continent, they are dependent upon one another for mass action. They must organize for a task so great as marketing their product. Individual farmers could not market California fruit in New York as the union of fruit growers can do. The results have been wonderful in the success attained in marketing the fruit and in the excellent prices secured by these Western farmers. The key to this success is the abolition of competitive cheating and trickery. The apples, for instance, in the Hood Valley, Oregon, are packed by a committee. No individual farmer manages the preparation of his own apples for market. The committee is cold and impartial, and cares only for the proper grading of the fruit and the securing of a buyer through reliable and fair packing. The product is so uniform and the quality of the fruit can be relied on so generally that a higher price is paid for a box of apples from the Pacific Coast in the New York market than is paid for a barrel of apples from New York State itself.

A More Complete Example. The experience of economic federation in the United States has been so rare among country people that it has as many critics as it has advocates. The places are too few, the federations of farmers too remote from one another for their influence to be very great. The experience of Denmark stands forth in our time as the great example of the federation of country people under religious stimulus, in the interest of the whole people. I am indebted for these facts, which have not been adequately published in English, to Professor Fred Rasmussen, of the New Hampshire State College of Agriculture.

A Transformed Denmark. Denmark is a country twice the size of Massachusetts, having two and a half million people. Its leading industry is dairying. By 1864 the soil was depleted of fertility through the selling of grain from the land. The country had suffered defeat in war, lost the provinces of Schleswig-Holstein, and was under a heavy indemnity. To-day Denmark is the most productive of European countries and has the highest per capita wealth in Europe. " In Denmark," says Professor Rasmussen, " there are only a few who have too much, and still fewer who have too little."

The secret of this national prosperity is education, coöperation, and a strong national spirit pervading the whole population.

Value of Homogeneous Stock. The people are naturally organized by the fact that they are all of one national stock. The example of Denmark is significant in America, because in America the people on the farms are mostly American. The foreign population is coming into the cities but the country population is American-born with conspicuous and well-known exceptions. Indeed, the foreigners who are tilling the soil are more inclined to coöperation than the Americans themselves. But Denmark having a homogeneous, native-born, country population of a strong independent type, has been able, because of their consciousness of kind, to organize coöperation among country people. What I am to describe concerns the rural, and not the urban, populations of Denmark.

Range of Organization. Natural organization, steadily growing, has developed into a Central Co-operative Committee of Denmark. Under this national organization there are coöperative societies for production, as for instance cattle breeding associations. There are coöperative societies for manufacture of country products into commodities, as the manufacture of pork into bacon and of milk into butter and cheese. These processes in Denmark are in the hands of the farmers themselves. There are coöperative societies for the protection of health, of saving, and of credit, and there are societies which coöperate in the active brotherhood of man.

Altruistic Feature. Denmark has live stock gatherings, societies for protecting poor men, who have but one horse or one cow, against loss. Some well-to-do farmers belong to these societies in order to help the community. Insurance is secured by coöperation. These small coöperative bodies have members who never draw their benefits, but belong to the society in order to help the community. There are small banks in Denmark which have only one man on salary. The president of the bank receives $150 per year, while directors serve in turn without pay.

Sanitariums Secured. This spirit in Denmark is far from being commercial; it is at once religious, humane, and patriotic. The recent discovery that tuberculosis can be cured in its early stages occasioned a great movement in Denmark to provide sanitariums for the cure of consumption. A general organization under the leadership of ministers and philanthropists secured contributions for this purpose from all parts of the kingdom, and so general was the response, so small the gifts, that some coöperative Bacon Associations contributed as little as eighty-one cents. A Creamery Association was solicited to contribute five cents per year for twenty years, for each cow, which was equivalent to one pint of milk per cow per year. The movement for the cure of consumptives was on this basis successful, and adequate sanitariums were provided out of these small gifts, universally contributed; but the coöperative organization of Denmark was essential to this result.

Idea of Collective Success. In Denmark tag days are general, celluloid flowers being used instead of unsightly labels. Coöperation is based on a sense of the common good and the distribution of the strain according to the amount of business done in the community, and on a spirit of helpfulness as opposed to selfishness. The Danes have a sense that success is not individual, but that it is the common prosperity of all the members of the community.

Sources Defined. Professor Rasmussen says that the sources of this national coöperation in Denmark are, first, the natural growth of a people who are akin to one another. The second cause is the educational system, which all observers of Denmark say is stimulated by religious motives. The third working cause in Denmark is the national songs of the country. These are heard outside the city. They are rural songs of the woods, of the brooks, of the birds, and of the fields. And, fourthly, the students in the schools of Denmark are the apostles of the nationalist movement. They are the teachers of coöperation and they work in this cause without pay.

Inclusive and Intense Character. Teachers in Denmark are cared for. The public quickly responds to their needs. There is a legal department in these coöperative systems which serves those who need, free of charge. Information and instruction are constantly being imparted to the people, and the result is a passionate sense of common adversity and common effort.

Lines of Encouragement. I am frequently asked whether the country Church in America can ever succeed, whether the people will ever return to the country in sufficient numbers to make it a powerful institution, competent to meet the needs of American country life. The answer is found in Denmark and in Ireland. For these two countries are meeting under the guidance of consecrated men the problems of their people. Ireland is getting rid of her beggars, Denmark has abolished pauperism and closed her poorhouses, and is building churches. The answer to this question is found in populations of the United States, who even now, in scientific application of country life in the federation of their institutions and coöperation in securing a livelihood, are maintaining themselves against all adverse change.

Worth of Religious Idealism. In all these cases of successful country life, the influence of religion and of a passionate idealism is evident. The Church is the farmer's source of idealism. Country people have not many institutions, nor will they ever have; therefore the place of the Church is a great one and the spirit of the Church should be coöperative: the organizations of the Church should be federated. There must be in such a coöperative life of the farmers the beginning of religious coöperation.

The opportunity for preaching a common gospel among the farmers thus united is very great, for the economic experience enters largely into religious thought.

Call for Religious Sacrifice. But it must not be inferred that without religious sacrifice these results in federation can be easily reaped. Religious people who believe in federation must be prepared to make sacrifices for it. It is a doctrine with stern implications, and when all its meaning is known there will be many not ready to strip themselves of that which they value or to consecrate their preferences to the common gain of the Kingdom.

Quaker Hill Community Church. The writer was a minister at Quaker Hill, New York. The community was made up of many groups of members and adherents of different denominations. When a church was to be formed he asked of his own denomination to be ordained with the understanding that the church thus formed would not be of his denomination nor of any other. After much debate this request was granted and he was ordained for the formation of a church from which his own denominational name was to be excluded. At its organization the five near-by congregations, all of them, except one, located in other communities, were asked to send minister and delegate to approve the independent church to be formed on Quaker Hill. One of these was the Quaker Meeting, in whose territory the new church was about to be formed. This Quaker Meeting sent as its representative an aged elder, Richard Osborn, whose saintly life and stern nobility of character were the mainstay of the declining Meeting, in which his fathers had for almost two generations worshiped.

Personal Sacrifice Shown. The Baptist minister invited to this organization of an independent church had by his preaching converted many of the members of the proposed church. He came to the meeting, with explicit protest and with great sacrifice of his own feelings, and impelled by a sense of duty to the community, in which he had preached the gospel with power and tenderness. He came because he loved the members of the church and could not refuse. He was appointed to give the right hand of fellowship to the new church, and did so with grace and fervor. The old Quaker elder near the close of the meeting, when all " sat in silence," arose and in words of inexpressible dignity and sweetness welcomed the new church into the community, which had been served by the Quakers alone for two centuries. Richard Osborn knew when he so spoke that at his death the Meeting which he loved would be " laid down." He was passing on the mantle of the old Quaker preachers to the officers of the new church. Into this church were received adherents of eleven denominations.

Compromise of Principles not Required. This story is told in order to illustrate the sacrifices

which Christian people must make if they are to
have federation; whatever is demanded for the
sake of a united community must be done, so long
as it involves no sacrifice of the spiritual welfare
of people now living in that community. If you
believe in federation, you must believe in the people
whose hearts God has touched more than you believe in the peculiar doctrines which have pleased
and convinced yourself. The common and universal
beliefs of Christian people are enough for any man
who would be united in a noble Christianity.
Whatever sacrifice is demanded of a Christian in a
community must be made that the whole community
may be one. This can be done without essential
compromise of principles. If the spirit be Christian
and if the devotion of the man be a uniting experience, he can let his preferences be known without
offense. The example of his self-sacrifice in lay-
ing them aside for the sake of the community will
be the more impressive.

Federation a Present Ideal. On the whole very
little is being done throughout the United States
in the federation of churches. It is an ideal of
men rather than a practise. Probably in the future it will be seen that our discussion of federation
to-day was preliminary to a great religious movement, the end of which we cannot now see. Nearly
everybody professes to believe in it, with sincerity,
but the difficulties are so many and the path of action
is so obscure that results are not obtained.

Definite Progress in Maine. In the State of

Maine, where the Protestant churches have a homogeneous population and the whole State has a certain unity, federation of churches has had a definite success, and, within limits, a power and an efficiency little known elsewhere. Leadership is a large factor in this success, for the State has a few recognized leaders whose voice is heard by all men. Conspicuous among these is President William DeWitt Hyde, of Bowdoin College. The proposal of federation came from a Methodist minister and all denominations of Protestants are united. So well established has the work of this federation become that communities which find themselves in need of uniting their churches are able to request the kindly offices of the federation and to promise obedience to its mandates. On the proper occasion the officers of the federation come to the community, study the situation, and determine upon an arrangement of the churches. Sometimes an individual church must go out of existence, and the federation decides which one shall be abandoned. The rural population of Maine is in many communities less than in former years and fewer churches are needed. Moreover, the people are more united in spirit than they were, so that the federation corresponds to the changes in population and in social feeling. General obedience to the decision of the federation and respect for its high purposes have resulted, in the course of its history.

Outlook of New England Federation. The New

England Federation of Churches under the leadership of the Rev. E. Tallmadge Root, Secretary, is doing valuable service in bringing the churches of Massachusetts and Rhode Island to a sense of their common duty to the community. It is holding constantly before the churches the ideal of united service to the whole people.

Federal Council of Churches. The Federal Council of the Churches of Christ in America is a union of leading Protestant denominations in the interest of American religious life. It is important that there be such a center, as a clearinghouse of information, as headquarters for reference in the inquiries that bear upon the mutual relations of the churches, for the Federal Council can act as a mediary between denominations when they incline toward union. It does also great service in organizing local federations of States and of counties.

Federation by Counties. In certain counties of Pennsylvania the unit for federated action has been found to be not the community in which are a number of separate churches, but the county. The reason given is that the county is more neutral. It is neither a conference, nor an association, nor a diocese, nor a presbytery, but it is a civil division, corresponding in extent to any one of these districts. The relation of church federation to public reform, to public sanitation, and to the humane interests of the churches, suggests that the county be the unit in federating the churches. This movement in Pennsylvania has gone far enough to show that it is on right lines. The experience of the ministers in working together brings forth results, but slowly. Sentiment is growing, and the basis of procedure seems to be a correct one.

An Ideal Gradually to be Realized. Above all, it must be borne in mind that federation is an ideal. It grows out of the situation of modern life. It must be cherished with reserve and at the same time with emphasis. It has great promise for the future, though very often it seems impracticable in the present. Because the community cannot work in the federation there is no reason why the minister and leading Christian people shall not advocate it. In time the change will come. It is well that it should not come too soon. Those who have known how great is the cost of uniting denominations are in no hurry to precipitate the difficulties and the bitter costs of such a movement. What we need above all is the experience of working together. Christian people must work and pray, their ministers must preach, and the teaching of their leaders must be to the end that all Christians may be one. This is the path in which we are going. It is written large upon the future and it is bursting in hope and aspiration from the hearts of the best people in the churches. When the time comes it will appear as the kingdom of God does, without observation. But in that coming there are to be great sacrifices and profound changes in the life, in the thought, and the feeling of Christian people.

POVERTY AND PROSPERITY

Next to war, pestilence, and famine, the worst thing that can happen to a rural community is absentee landlordism. In the first place, the rent is all collected and sent out of the neighborhood to be spent somewhere else; but that is the least of the evils. In the second place, there is no one in the neighborhood who has any permanent interest in it except as a source of income. The tenants do not feel like spending any time or money in beautification, or in improving the moral or social surroundings. Their one interest is to get as large an income from the land as they can in the immediate present. Because they do not live there, the landlords care nothing for the community, except as a source of rent, and they will not spend anything in local improvements unless they see that it will increase rent. Therefore such a community looks bad, and possesses the legal minimum in the way of schools, churches, and other agencies for social improvement. In the third place, and worst of all, the landlords and tenants live so far apart and see one another so infrequently as to furnish very little opportunity for mutual acquaintance and understanding. Therefore class antagonism arises, and bitterness of feeling shows itself in a variety of ways. Where the whole neighborhood is made up of a tenant class which feels hostile toward the absent-landlord class, evasions of all kinds are resorted to in order to beat the hated landlords. On the other hand, the landlords are goaded to retaliation, and the rack-rent system prevails. Sometimes the community feeling among tenants becomes so strong as to develop a kind of artificial " tenant right," which is in opposition to the laws of the land, and the laws of the land are then made more severe in order to control the " tenant right."—*Thomas Nixon Carver*

POVERTY AND PROSPERITY

Increasing Proportion of Poor. The increase in
the number of industrious poor weighs heavily
upon the minds of Christian people. Not only is
the number increased of those who are poor, but
the proportion in the population appears to be
greater than it was. This increase came to attention at the very time when the free lands in the
United States were exhausted. For while there
are still some homesteads to be given away or sold,
their influence upon the life of the country is not
what it was. We are at the end of the period of
the influence of free land upon our racial stock.
It is striking now to discover that millions of people
in America are without land and without productive
tools.

Term Defined. To be poor, in the meaning of
this chapter, is to be landless and without productive tools. We are not concerned here with
the tramp or the outcast, important as their cases
are, but with society itself and with the community,
in which is discovered a large essential factor consisting of persons who do not own productive land
or tools. These I call poor, because with no land
and no capital they are unable to resist the strain

of want and it is easy for them to be plunged into pauperism. Their life is one of struggle. They are breadwinners. Very many of them are dependent upon wages. In the country they are tenant farmers or " renters," who are striving generally to possess land. In the cities they are clerks and working men and women who work for hire, having no ownership in productive industry.

Tenant Farmers in Productive States. It is amazing that fifty per cent. of the people in the open country, in the wealthiest farming States, are without land and do not own the tools by which the land is tilled. They are tenant farmers. The proportion of these tenants is shown by the last census [1] to have greatly increased in the States in which the soil is richest. Moreover, in these States the proportion of tenants is greater in those counties where the soil is most productive, and smaller in the counties where the soil is poorer.

Diminished Number in New England. In the New England States, whose soil has been depleted, the proportion of tenant farmers has diminished in the past ten years. Now the religious approach to a renter is different from the approach to an owner of land. He looks upon life in a wholly different way, and religion is so intimate to the experiences of men that it takes a different form in the man who is poor, that is, economically dependent. He does not think as the landowner does, nor feel as he feels.

[1] Census of 1910.

Southern Landholders and Tenants. Principal Webb, the famous master of the fitting school at Bellebuckle, Tennessee, described this condition to me in some such terms as this: " The old-style Southern farmer was a landholder. He had books and read them. He sent his son to college, and he supported the Church. But the modern farmer in the Southern States is close. He holds to every dollar with jealous care. He buys no books. His children do not seek higher education. He is eager to own land and to buy more land." The tenant farmer has become the type of countryman in many of these Southern States. In Georgia, Mississippi, Alabama, and Louisiana the proportion of tenant farmers is between fifty and sixty per cent. In Tennessee the renters, as they are called in the South, are one half of the country population.

Determining Factor in Problem. It is not my present concern to picture the condition of economic dependence, except as it is found in the open country, but to show that it is the cause which is changing the religious and political and educational complexion of the cities as well. The poor are multiplying about the churches, and with their large proportions they have become the determining factor in public and social work throughout the country.

Duty Required at Present. These increases in the proportion of those who are dependent on others for land and for tools is most marked in the wealthiest parts of the country. In the States which are stored with the greatest potential wealth, as

New York, Pennsylvania, Illinois, and Colorado, the proportions of the poor are the greatest. This is the most discouraging and burdensome fact of all. I intend to offer no solution of it. It is for Christian people to serve, while this condition prevails, as Christ would serve such a people according to their needs.

Apparently Permanent Condition. So far as we can now see, these conditions are permanent. Their causes are established. Men differ as to the remedy. Until they can agree and we may unite in a statesmanship which will distribute the wealth of the country among the people, it is the duty of Christians to think and serve and work for the poor. The forces which perpetuate this condition are essential to our life. We know no better way of life than the American way. Many of those who are without land and without tools become well-to-do, and some have become rich; but nevertheless the numbers of the poor are as great, and the proportions of the poor are increasing. So long as America is a prosperous country it will be filled in the cities and out in the open country with incoming streams of immigration from poorer lands. As long as our richest lands can be used to remedy this condition, they will be exploited by increasing proportions of breadwinners, of whom the most will fill the ranks of the working poor.

Religious Abolition of Poverty. Jesus said, " Blessed are ye poor, for yours is the kingdom of God." What did he mean? It does not seem so to

us. His meaning is not a part of our philosophy of
life. It is not an American way of looking at
things. Was he right, and if so, was he right only
for Syria and for Palestine? Is poverty in
America a religious condition? I want in this
chapter to show that in the country community
poverty can be under the control of the community
and pauperism can be abolished. The process of
lifting any population out of poverty is for them a
religious experience. I do not speak of the individual. For a man to get rich often means for
him to lose his religion; but for a whole people to
be lifted out of poverty by a gain that is distributed
through the number, is usually in history an experience attended with religious gains. For a community or a commonwealth to keep all of its members out of poverty and to care for its poor, is a
religious experience. Indeed the most tenacious
and valuable religious experience we have had in
the country is among those people who have cared
for their poor, have fought the battle against pauperism in the interest of their weaker members, and
have built up a way of life for the people as a
whole in which the blighting and destroying effects
of poverty shall not be felt.

Protestant Developments from Poverty. As a
matter of history, all the Protestant denominations,
except two, have grown out of the condition
of poverty. The various branches of the Presbyterian, Reformed, Methodist, and Baptist churches
in the United States, as also the Quakers and the

various Mennonite churches, such as the Dunkers and the Amish, have all come from populations which were poor together, and their religious life has been enjoyed along with the betterment of their condition. They have gotten a better livelihood as they matured and elaborated their religious systems. The Wesleys preached to people in England who were so poor that the Church of England would not have them, but John Wesley while he lived commented on the economic improvement of his people, and once he humorously said, " I cannot keep my Methodists poor."

Marginal People Determine Type of Community Life. Moreover the religious character of poor people who are saved from pauperism is shown in this that the people without lands and without tools are the marginal people of the community, and upon them the standards of moral and religious feeling in the community rest. Their way of living fixes the standard for the community. It is not to be expected that higher standards will prevail throughout the community than they can attain to. This is the reason why in New York City the problems of the tenement-house are the problems of the whole city. Not everybody lives in a tenement in New York, but people who live in private houses cannot be sure that their children will be more healthy, or more moral, or more spiritual than the people who live in the tenement-house may be: the moral standards of the tenement-house prevail throughout the whole city. This is the reason why

the mill-worker is so important in the community
life of Pittsburgh. The well-to-do people of Pittsburgh are many and excellent, but the standards of
moral feeling and of religious experience which
prevail among the mill-workers influence the people
of the whole city.

Working People Fix the Outlook. In the country
community the tenant farmer determines the standards of conduct for the community. Of course a
few will always be better than he, but I am speaking
in social terms, and social conditions are not made
up of the few. The average child in the country
community is more under the influence of the tenant
farmer and the conditions of the tenant farmer's
house, than he is of his own household, no matter
how well born he be. The essential problems of
the working people of any community must be
regarded as vital problems of the whole community.

Relation to Faith. If this is true, then poverty
is a religious condition, and they who have been
poor, who have lived for years without knowledge
of the future, who have no store of goods to live
upon, know that faith in God is the faith of the
Twenty-third Psalm, and they know that dependence upon God for daily supply is the beginning of
religious experience. The anxieties of the family
as to the future and as to the clothing and education of their children, as to those things necessary for self-respect, are the sources of religious
experience and of the belief in God. This is why

Jesus said, " Blessed are ye that hunger now, for ye shall be filled."

Making Ideals Effective. " If there is a new birth in the Church," says Dr. Edward T. Devine, head of the Charity Organization Society of New York City, " it will deal with poverty, not alone through deacons' and orphan alms, though these have their place, but by developing throughout the membership of the Church the ideal of a Christian community in which chronic poverty, like professional crime, will have disappeared." [1] On another page of the same book he says, " Poverty can be abolished and permanent progress cannot be made until it is."

Challenge to the Churches. What a challenge to the churches is this from the same writer, whose splendid faith in the power of religion is unshaken in the midst of the misery of a great city! " Preventable disease, probably not less than one half of all the disease which we now have, and preventable accidents, probably two thirds of those which we now have, will certainly disappear, when as the result of the spiritual awakening in the churches, there is a private and a public conscience which will deal with their causes."

Quaker Ability to Fight Poverty. The difference between the country and the city is most marked in the greater ability of the country community, as shown in American history, to deal with poverty. The country life movement will contribute

[1] *Social Forces,* 90, 206, 207.

a priceless gift to the future if it leads men to imitate successfully these country communities which have saved their people from pauperism; for this the cities have not done. The Quaker settlements in the country have known how to fight the battle with pauperism. For a century and a half certain Quaker communities have maintained themselves in the country and none among them has suffered from poverty. This has not been due to their being uniformly rich, for the Quakers are subtly aristocratic, and marked differences prevail among them. But the whole community has been trained under the influence of the Meeting to care for their members who possess but one horse and one cow. Whenever at Quaker Hill a working man has lost his horse or cow or suffered through fire the loss of his house or barn, the whole community has responded and restored to him that which was lost. Thus for almost two centuries the whole population has been kept from pauperism.

Instance at Quaker Hill. This applies to the members of the community, whether Quakers or not. On this hilltop the population of Quakers is now small. About ten years ago an outsider secured the contract for delivering mail on Quaker Hill. He had not yet begun to take the profits of his contract when one of his horses died. These horses were his productive tools. Within a very short time the whole community by apparently spontaneous action had subscribed the money to buy him a horse. The influence of this act in welding the community into one was almost incredible. Its effect upon the recipient himself need not be described.

Pennsylvania German Communal Success. " The Pennsylvania Germans " are a group of populations religiously organized, who had their sources among the poor of Europe, at the time of the Reformation. The leading influence among them is the Mennonite way of life from which the Quakers' mode of life is derived. They have the same methods of extinguishing pauperism. These methods have now become instinctive and they apply to all residents in the community, whether members of the Meeting or not. The religious genius of the Mennonites and the Quakers has recognized that " the injury of one is the concern of all."

Contrast with New England. Contrast this dealing with poverty to methods which have prevailed in New England, where with all the sense of the community, as expressed in the Town Meeting, the poor were neglected. The genius of New England has been to emphasize the success of leading citizens. All the community's oil was put in the lamp of the boy who went to college. The man who became rich, the deacon in the church, or any other person whose success in business, in scholarship, or in piety was eminent satisfied the mind of the New Englander, and the rest of the people were not regarded. The result has been that many of the New England stock have been neglected, the community has lost very often its ablest members and has been

proud of their departure into far-off eminence. But
the community has suffered through the weakness
of its poorer members and has gone down with
them, in obedience to the principle that the people
who are poor determine the moral and spiritual
standards of the community.

Must Guard People's Source of Income. We
have had in all the American population a devotion to the poor which is religious and educational,
but not economic. I am urging the sincere care of
the income of the poorer members. The community must see that they have enough to live on, and
that their sources of income are not impaired. It
is not sufficient that we preach the gospel to the
poor, and care nothing for their living. They will
not take from us the word of eternal life if we do
not guard their possession of a livelihood. The
beginning of the process of eternal life is the eating
of daily bread. We do not need to care for the
income of the well-to-do. There is nothing religious about the salary of a man who has ten
thousand dollars a year, but the income of a man
who never has more than one hundred dollars to
spare is a religious problem to him and to his
family and to the community.

Educational Measures not Enough. Educational
measures for the poor are not sufficient. The public school system, which is standardized so that the
child of the poorest can attend school and is
protected by law so that he must attend, does not
protect the community against poverty. We have

nothing within the educational system that leads a whole population into ownership of land and tools. Indeed the States in which the proportions of tenant farmers are increasing are the States with an excellent educational system and all the children of the people going to school.

Churches Built by Working Folk. Meantime the churches of the country are probably built, certainly their first structures were erected, out of the contributions of people many of whom never owned a thousand dollars. They are the folk who give for the establishment of religious institutions. They know the value of religion to themselves. They show by their gifts in the hardest situations of life, as on the frontier, that common religious experience is precious above all things. To no other social institution do they contribute so much and so universally as to the erection of churches and to the support of ministers.

A Church Losing Its Democratic Basis. Yet strange to say, the attention of churches is too frequently, after their earliest days, turned upon the few persons of means in their membership. I remember a church in Nebraska, standing on the rim of an unexplored prairie, which had but ten years of growth behind it, in which one man, giving five hundred dollars a year to the minister, was the controlling factor. The church had been erected by the homesteaders in the days of the bitter poverty of Nebraska, but soon it lost the democracy of its early methods and looked to the prosperous citizen for his gift, which, in spite of his wisdom and nobility of character, was corrupting and degrading to them.

Need of Church as a Training Center. The important principle in Church life throughout the country as a whole to-day is to make the Church a channel for consecrating the growing prosperity of the people. Poverty which is governed by the community, with pauperism excluded by the common action of the people, is a religious condition, but it is for the Church to organize this into a system of contribution, by which the people shall continue to give as they prosper. The Church will thus become the religious drill-ground of the whole population. They will learn in it the lessons of benevolence, of missionary giving, and of stewardship. Such a Church will train leaders in the great enterprises of the future. From such a Church will come the presidents of colleges and workers in the great charities, the millionaires who give in their abundance to splendid enterprises, and the philanthropists whose princely gifts will lead in solving the terrifying problems of the world.

Principle of Envelope System. This is the meaning of the envelope system of contributions, which does not standardize the gifts of the whole congregation upon the rich man who may pass away or who may do worse by remaining and controlling the church. The envelope gifts of all the people in the church look alike. Giving to the Lord by this method makes the passing of the plate a holy act, unsullied by envy and by shame. In a working community it is one of the most essential ways of securing the attendance of the poor at church. Congregations all over the United States are transforming their system of pew-rents into a system of envelope giving. This system must not be thought of as "businesslike" alone. It is a method in the administration of the churches which expresses a greater wisdom and a new devotion; for the people are prospering, even in the poverty which can give only through envelopes. The church is their common possession, and by this system the poor can give to the church in the same way as the widow gave to the temple, whose two mites were "all she had."

People Prizing a Common Project. A church in New York State, whose bills were all paid from an endowment, decided to turn to the support of a foreign missionary. Their pastor, who received nothing from them for his living, led them into giving to the support of a missionary board. The result of a canvass of the community in this interest was surprising to all. More people took part in this act of giving than in any other one collective act of the congregation. The list of givers to the salary in China was longer than the church-membership, larger than that of the Sunday-school, with the young people's societies combined. Everybody desired to have a hand in this community support of a missionary physician in China. The community itself was entering into the days of cash values. A profitable form of farming sustained country people there. They recognized their obligations to the Lord in the cheerful and hearty support of this common project.

Result of a Thorough Canvass. A Wisconsin minister began his pastorate on $450 per year. He did not tell the bride whom he asked to share this munificent living that one tenth of it was already promised to the Lord. Against her vociferous protest he paid his tithe during their first year. He went with equal vigor to his church officers and insisted that everybody in the congregation should be canvassed for an offering to the Lord; and when they after a feeble effort stopped short, he offered to their amazement to canvass the rest himself, and against their protest he did so, bringing in inside of a year so much as to increase his own salary and the missionary gifts of the church up to a scale of $1,600 a year. The principle on which this work was done was the frank, manly demand, " Pay to the Lord what you owe." Mr. Breeze pressed this demand so far as to go to Milwaukee and present himself at the office of the owner of a farm in his parish whose tenants worshiped in his church. He was rewarded with a generous yearly contribution.

A Gift Bringing Joy. Among his parishioners was a poor washerwoman who, when he asked her for a gift, burst into tears. Both she and the minister were from Wales and he spoke to her in the sweet tongue that touched her heart, telling her that he wanted her to give out of her poverty, and asking her if she could not give two cents a week. This she cheerfully promised, and the woman came to church. Her glowing face and fervor in the service, Sunday after Sunday, was due not to his sermons, but to her gift, for she knew that she was giving out of her poverty and struggle " all she had."

Response of Poor in St. George's. This is the secret of the administration of such parishes as St. George's in New York City, where the poor have been assembled in great congregations within the walls which before had congregations of two or three or five families. At one time this parish had seven thousand members, twenty-five hundred of whom lived east of Second Avenue, no one having an income of more than $15 per week, but every member of this church was accustomed to give. If he failed to put his weekly contribution in the plate, he received the same strict treatment as the richer man whose gift would seem more desirable. The nickels and dimes of the very poor were sought by this parish with the same thoroughness and valued as highly as the dollars and the thousands of dollars of the few rich members of the parish. This is what it means to put a spiritual value on money. The spiritual value is the community value. The church is built out of the sacred income of the poor. The income of poor people is always a sacred thing in the religion of the community.

Church Budget. A big problem in the religious administration of the life of poor people is to budget the church's financial burdens for the year in so far as the policy of the denomination will permit. At the beginning of any year let the officers of the church find out how much they need for local expenses, for benevolences, and for missionary gifts. Let this amount be distributed among the members of the church and congregation, assigning to each one what he probably ought to give, beginning with the poorest. Let the whole congregation then be canvassed and a contribution be secured from every member. It will be found that the gifts of the congregation will correspond in the total to the amount budgeted by the officers, and these gifts will come in regularly. The congregation will respond to a method which respects them and which unites them.

Duplex Envelope. For this purpose the duplex envelope is excellently suited. In one small envelope there are two pockets, one for local support and one for benevolences. The destination of these gifts can be printed on the outside; and for greater convenience, on the side of the flap, in order to avoid a mistake by the giver. This envelope is to be torn in two and the money for benevolences is given to its proper treasurer, and that for local support to the treasurer of the church. Out of this constant stream of small gifts the whole enterprise of the church can be carried on successfully.

Advantage of Budget System. One great advantage of this budget is that a church cannot be stampeded by some forcible speaker. The minister and officers know what they propose to do for that year and nomadic appeals of peripatetic advocates of special causes cannot be made, except to the officers themselves; who can grant out of the surplus of their budget a certain amount. If the giving of the congregation is consolidated, the people are federated in one act of benevolence. They are being trained in financing the kingdom of God. Their prosperity is under one common organizing principle.

Contributions According to Prosperity. It is essential to this method that the people give in accordance as they " may prosper." The officers of the church are the watchful guardians of the conscience of the people. It is their business to train the people in giving. They will know who has prospered and who has suffered. In their hands too, as the most fitting leaders, is the study of the great causes of the time and the determination to which of them that church shall give. Most people live their religious life within the bounds of the congregation in which they worship, and the officers become the watchmen on the tower of Zion, who direct the forces of the church toward the great enterprises of the Kingdom.

Ministers Should Have a Living Wage. The great problem in this new administration of the prosperity of the people is the supporting of ministers. The weakness, especially of country churches, is expressed in the fact that the ministers have not enough to live on. Of course there are a few men in country churches who have done heroically on $600 per year, but unfortunately their number is very small. The actual fact is that most of the men who live on six hundred or three hundred dollars a year and who continue to minister to the same people for as much as five years, are, as a result, not highly efficient. The uniting of financial and spiritual genius in one man is very uncommon. The churches cannot expect to find good ministers who could organize a successful department store. Ministers in the country ought to have a living wage. They have a right to ask no more, but they have a right to ask enough to keep the average man in ordinary comfort at the work required in that parish.

A Mechanic's Living Wage. Recent studies by the Russell Sage Foundation in New York State show that in the smaller communities of that State a mechanic, working at one of the trades, can live on $800 per year. In this standard of living are included sufficient food, housing, clothing, medical care, recreation, and other essentials of life, to keep a family of five. Below this amount it was discovered that family life degenerates, children become sickly, and death comes too often untimely. But at this standard it is believed a family of five can be expected to live.

Average Annual Pastoral Support. Our interest here is in the man employed by a religious body, namely, a minister of the gospel. Let us give him as good a living as a mechanic requires for bare subsistence. There are many country churches that do not pay so much to a minister. They may find, if they please, in this fact the reason why their ministers, if they are young men, leave them as soon as their children are born and begin to cost money, and why they can only expect to secure old men, without families to educate. Such churches above all others need the permanent services of ministers who can live with them at least five years or ten, and accomplish some cumulative and lasting work. Every church should pay to its minister every year of his work an amount sufficient for an average year of his life. No church ought to take a minister in his cheap years and let some other church support him in his expensive years. This is the way by which country churches exact " graft " of the town and city churches; and the punishment they deserve comes upon them, for they are the weaker and the town and city churches are the stronger. The strength of the church is not expressed in what the minister gives it, but in what it does for him and for the Kingdom.

Cost of Keeping a Horse. Taking now the minister who has as good housing and clothing and food and medical care as a mechanic, let us see what he needs to do the work that the mechanic is not called on to do. First of all, he must own a horse, which will cost him for keep $150 per year. The farmer's horse costs no such amount. A minister in the country had to spend $150 to $200 every year for

five years to keep his horse.   Except as a means of
serving his people, he had no need of a horse.   In
the same parish he now owns a farm on which he
keeps a horse; and he costs him from $25 to $50 per
year.   It is easy to see that the farmer in a community cannot understand why the minister's horse is
so expensive, for very few farmers know that their
own horses cost them anything, except the charge
by the blacksmith.   The minister has to pay cash
for everything.

Allowance for Books.   Now let us give this minister the tools of his trade; namely, books.   These
are as essential to him as the reaper and the hay-
rake are to the farmer.   They have the same place in
his occupation as the corn-planter has with the
Illinois farmer.   They economize his work and enable him to cultivate the soil of modern minds.   If
he has not books, his people will not long hear him.
It is his business to know the books of the world and
to convey to his people the great thoughts of great
souls.   Let us give the minister, therefore, $50 per
year for books.   He is a very poor tiller of the souls
of his parish, if he does not read one book a week at
a cost of one dollar per week.

Income for Old Age.   The income for old age
should be provided for in the budget of a minister.
He must not be looking out for good investments or
spending his time speculating in land.   " They that
proclaim the gospel should live of the gospel."   I do
not think a minister in a country community ought
to be obliged to keep even a garden, but that is a

matter of opinion and personal fitness. It is all-essential that he should till the soil of his people's minds, and if he does that, some one else can raise the vegetables. So that against old age he must be protected by $100 per year in his economic scale, from the time of his ordination at twenty-five to the day of his retirement at sixty-five. This investment will support a man and wife comfortably in their declining years.

Education of Children. The children of the minister should be educated as well as their parents. The universal feeling of all kinds of folk is, that their children should be trained to know as much as their parents and to do as well. To educate the children of a Protestant minister will require $100 per year for each child from its birth until it is of age. In our estimate let us allow $300 for the average Protestant minister's family.

Summary of Expenditures. Now to add up all these details: $800 enables the minister to live as well as the working man who can barely subsist, with health and unimpaired vigor, in the State of New York; $150 for a horse; $50 for books; $100 for old age; and $300 for the education of children, we have a total of $1,400 per year.

Estimate of Marriage Fees and Donations. Allowance in this budget must be made for marriage fees and donations in the minister's income. In the country the minister may receive from marriage fees fifty to one hundred dollars and from donations as much more. In a generous parish, where many

farmers not members of any church desire to contribute to the minister's living, the total of these
donations in a year amounted to $40. The diffi-
culty in reckoning such gifts in the budget is that
year by year as farming becomes more systematic
their total amount decreases. Though the number
of donations is as great as ever, their value to the
minister is much less than of old. Moreover, the
donation is a tradition, but country life has many
new families who do not know the old ways, and
they give nothing. I would estimate, therefore, the
donations and marriage fees at a sum not in excess
of one hundred to one hundred and fifty dollars
per year. There is no recorded instance in which the
donations and fees have been so large in recent
years as to detain a minister in the country when
his salary was insufficient for his support.

No Allowance for Travel. If he makes no investments and secures wealth from no other source,
as he should not do, if he is dependent upon his people to whom he ministers in spiritual things, $1,400
is what he actually spends year after year if he keeps
a horse, uses books, has three children, and grows
old in serving a country parish. This allows nothing for travel, nothing for cultivating those sources
of thought and feeling which will be helpful to his
people through the attendance upon conventions and
other public gatherings. But he is doing work that
costs him year after year the amount named. Now
it is the difference between this amount and the
average country minister's salary that is the main

cause for the constant movement of country ministers from place to place.

Motives that Cause Changes. The one motive which above all other things causes him " to seek a new call " is the desire to educate his children, and to secure enough to live on. The anxiety in regard to old age is an increasing force in this dire process, as years pass; and when the minister comes to be forty he adopts new measures for the years which he sees before him of declining power and efficiency. It is useless to argue that ministers should live on less. The important thing is to provide that which will enable them, and will content them, to live in country places. The experience of the churches shows that in country communities where the minister is sufficiently well paid a sufficient supply of good men can always be secured and retained.

Farmers More Prosperous. The importance of this matter grows upon modern people with the increasing prosperity of country communities. Farmers who have tilled the soil with difficulty and made a poor living for a good part of a lifetime, have in recent years largely prospered. " I have made more money in the past three years than in all my farming before," said a farmer of forty-four years of age recently, and all over the United States farmers are facing the better prospect which is before their industry.

Scientific Management will Increase Profits. Moreover the methods made valuable from scientific agriculture are now seen to contain vast potential

THOROUGHBRED STOCK ON A MODERN FARM

wealth for the farmer. Depleted soils are being restored, and although a period of poverty and struggle will be necessary in restoring them, their future is one of great wealth, and permanent tillage of these soils under scientific management promises cumulative gains. Coöperation among farmers is seen to be profitable. Some of those who are coöperating in America are so prosperous that their leaders fear for the result. I would not exaggerate this prosperity, for I know that it has sharp limitations at present, but we know the way by which the farmer shall prosper in the future. Already many have realized great gains. The consecration of this prosperity is the immediate task of the country Church.

Message in Terms of Experience. We are in the midst of a period of speculative farming. This means the turning of agricultural values for the time being into cash, the buying and selling of many farms, and the redistribution of land. Let us understand this process and speak to the present-day countryman in terms of his own immediate experience. Only thus will we minister to him in the things of God. Like the old evangelist, let the modern church " speak to their condition."

Rural Population Decreasing. Life in the open country will always be attenuated so far as we can now see. Indeed, there are those who say that the country should be robbed of its institutions and the life of country people centered in the towns. This I do not believe, but there is no evidence at present of an increase of the country population. The rural exodus is still going on and it is the opinion of such observers as L. H. Bailey that it will continue even further to diminish the numbers of people in the country. Among them the institutions will be few, but they ought to be powerful.

Magnify the Church. The Church and the school must always be in the country, if the people are there. All the greater should be the Church and all the more influential the school. The life of common folk in the laborious and difficult task of successful agriculture should be dignified with great and beautiful churches. Magnify the Church. Write its name large, not small. Think of it in terms of the whole community. Make it the dignifying building in the whole landscape of country life. Put the leadership of it in the hands of the strongest men and furnish them with the fuel for their fires and the oil for their engines. Assemble the people in great congregations, not in small, and make the Church the expression of the large things in the life of the people, a contrast very often to many of the detailed and intricate and annoying trifles which wear the life out of the farmer. Let the Church express the idealism of the farmer, and in order to do this the leading people of the country community must give very largely of their means and all the people of the community must consecrate unto the Lord what they have to give, as he has prospered them.

THE PRINCIPLE OF SERVICE

The ideal solution of the country Church problem is to have in each rural community one strong church adequately supported, properly equipped, ministered to by an able man—a church which leads in community service. The path to the realization of such an ideal is rough and thorny. Church federation, however, promises large results in this direction and should be especially encouraged. . . . Furthermore, there is supreme necessity for adding dignity to the country parish. Too often at present the rural parish is regarded either as a convenient laboratory for the clerical novice, or as an asylum for the decrepit or inefficient. The country parish must be a parish for our ablest and strongest. The ministry of the most Christlike must be to the hill towns of Galilee as well as to Jerusalem.—*K. L. Butterfield*

Let no one suppose that philanthropy is the chief medicine for the social ill health of the country. The intelligent student who possesses the true spirit of helpfulness may find in the rural problem ample scope for both his brain and his heart. But he will make a fundamental and irreparable error if he starts out with the notion that pity, charity, and direct gifts win the day. You may flatter the American farmer; you cannot patronize him. He demands and needs, not philanthropy, but simple justice, equal opportunity, and better facilities for education. He is neither slave nor pauper.—*K. L. Butterfield*

VII

THE PRINCIPLE OF SERVICE

Social Service Defined. After one of the great Protestant bodies had determined upon the principles of social service as its ideal for the future, and had passed the most elaborate statements, calling upon all its people to engage in social service, the presiding officer turned to a friend and said, " What is social service? " The answer to this question is the present task of the Christian student and worker. Social service is the ministry of a man, or group of men to a society. It may not be social service to lift a man who has fallen. It is not social service to lend money to a poor acquaintance. Such acts are personal services. Altruism is not social service. There are many personal services rendered in the world in which Christian folk are well trained, and an atmosphere of genial altruism prevails in our time. It is an enjoyable experience to give a little money to a beggar. People in the cities have to be trained and educated to resist the impulse to give in a random way to individuals in apparent need. This, however, is not social service. We are confronted with needy societies of men. Of course I do not mean lodges, or clubs, or other artificial organizations, but essential and instinctive societies, in which the life of men is immersed.

Service of Groups. As the fish lives in the pond or as the apple lives on the tree, so every man lives in a society. The smallest society of all is the household, and the greatest is the nation. Cities are societies, and the country community is a society, because in it an individual can pass the round of his life from birth to death. Social service is usually an act of an organization or group of men. An individual alone is usually inadequate to serve a society. He must have the support and allegiance of others in an organized group. For this reason men organize churches, charities, schools, and city governments, in order that groups of men may through teamwork minister to societies. The school-teacher who comes into a community serves through an organization, and represents a group of people devoted to the problem of education. The pastor who ministers to a country community is strengthened by the allegiance of his fellow-officers and of the denomination behind him, of which the symbols are in his ordination and installation. They fortify him for his service and his leadership of that people.

Serving Marginal People. To serve a society is not a quantitative matter. It is not like packing apples, or shoveling coal, in which every apple and every lump of coal must be handled uniformly. The first thing to learn in social service is selection. Most of the people in a society do not need to be approached. We serve a society by helping the

PRESBYTERIAN CHURCH, CAZENOVIA, NEW YORK

DR. PERSONS, THE PASTOR, REACHES THE COUNTRY SECTIONS BY
EVANGELISM

marginal people in that society, to help whom is the benefit of all. These are the children and youth, the working men, the " renters," and in general, the poor, the sick, and those who are about to die. Marginal people are the people on the edge of the society, who must struggle to maintain themselves in it. Those who are well-to-do or well fixed do not need to be served. It is their business to support the community leader: and if he makes good among marginal people, they will gladly sustain him. For social instinct and a sense of social unity command them.

The Marginal Conscience. All organized things are valued by their marginal parts. The economists say that wages are fixed in every scale of pay by estimating the value to the employer of the last man he hires, the man who is just productive enough to stay in the shop. Other men who produce more create the employer's profit, but they get no more pay than the man whose work is just good enough to be tolerated. He is the marginal man in the factory. The same applies in moral and spiritual affairs. The working man or half-grown boy in the town has the marginal conscience of the town. His ways of looking at things are the most contagious, and his experiences are the common experiences of the town; he has the price mark on him.

General Application of Principle. This principle has a very general application. If you are going to paint a view of the ocean, you will sit down on the shore and picture on your canvas the margin of the ocean. There are only a very few pictures of the ocean that represent the waves as seen from a ship. The literature of love represents marginal love, the affection of those about to be married. There are very few books on the profound and vital experiences of married folk. The State has to deal with conduct on its margins, where orderly behavior breaks down in crime. The State has very little to do with well-behaved people, but with those who get into trouble the State deals by means of the policeman and the court. The public values learning, not by the few men who are encyclopedic, but the common measure of learning is in the amount that an ordinary student can master. The unit of measure in education is the student, not the professor. Industry is valued in the churches of our time, not any longer in terms of millionaires or any other rich men, but of the working man. The problem of industrial life for which the public cares is the problem of the poor. This was not always so. The difference is in this, that in former times we had plenty and there need be none poor. In our day we are confronted with a struggle for subsistence on the part of most of our people.

Christ and Marginal People. The central concern of society, under the influence of Christ, is with those people who have the struggle. Christ always worked among the poor, and endured much opposition in order to do so. He clearly understood what he was about. His policy was deliberate. When the excellent people of his time, good substantial Pharisees, whose lives were orderly and comfortable, objected to his selection of marginal people as his daily companions, he defended himself. He interpreted social service, in the fifteenth chapter of Luke, in three short stories. He declared that these illustrate the mind of God. Each of them is a story about a little society, and he declared that the marginal unit set the value on all the other units in the society.

Principles Illustrated. One society was a flock of sheep. He declared that when one sheep is lost the value of all the rest is measured in the shepherd's mind by the lost one, and he takes no rest until he has found the marginal sheep. In the household the savings of the mother were ten pieces of money. When she lost one she set no store by the others until she found that one. Their value was measured in her mind by the one marginal piece. The third society was a gentleman's estate, and the whole story of this house is expressed in the prodigal conduct of one of the sons. In the mind of the father nothing else was of concern until his boy who was lost was found. The heart of the family estimated all things by the marginal son.

Organizations for Children and Youth. In early country life in America there were no marginal people, because there was no organic society. Household farming was the beginning of organized country life. In that day everybody had land. The service of the Church must be not to the poor, for there should be no poor—people who were in need were supposed to be shiftless. The Church therefore organized its ministries to the children and adolescent youth of the households. That period from 1800 to 1890 was the classic period in the development in American churches of Sunday-schools, which culminated in the young people's societies of Christian Endeavor, Baptist Unions, Epworth Leagues, and similar organizations expressive of the Church's joy in her young people. It was an organization of marginal people under the shelter of the Church, but they were the marginal people of the household societies.

Church Facing New Problems. In the past twenty years the churches have become concerned about communities. Without forgetting the household, the heart of the Church has been enlarged to take in a whole community. In the open country speculative farming has seriously affected the household. It has prepared the way for community life. A new figure has come into the concern of the Church in our day. In the cities the churches are facing the working man and his problems. In the country the churches are confronted with the tenant farmer. These are new types of households in the country. They look upon life in the marginal way. They are as different from landowners and from the owners in business as children are from parents or as the youth is from the elderly man. They are the marginal people, whom to serve is to serve the whole community.

Ministering in Common Things.   The great danger of the teacher, the pastor, the churchworker, is that he will be too nice, too scholastic, and too much concerned with rare and curious things.   Service of the community is concerned with common things. These common things make up the life of marginal people.   The church visitor goes to a mechanic's household, talks about children, sickness, wages, old age, savings, love and hate and fear, and other great common experiences of mankind.   When she goes to the home of a wealthy man for dinner the conversation is about automobiles, aëroplanes, foreign travel, the latest books, rare furniture, paintings, fine linen, and fashions.   These are all rare and curious things.   The reason why we incline to talk about them is partly in the fact that they are uncommon, and most people do not have access to them.   Man inclines to have things peculiar to himself and his little set of folk.

Jesus Ministered to Poor.   But in the rich man's house the things of concern in the poor man's house are also talked about.   These are common experiences.   Everything said at the poor man's table has equal value at the rich man's table, because sickness and children and old age and hate and fear and love are common human experiences.   The life of the poor man is made up of common things, the things which are universal, because the poor man is the marginal man.   He has the moral and spiritual price mark on him.   He is the standard of human value. That is the reason why Jesus devoted his life to the poor, because by working for the poor he could work for all mankind. Whatever is done in terms of the common, that is, marginal life, is done for the whole community.

Service to Landless People. In the period of speculative farming the marginal people are the poor. Capital is the determining standard and the people without capital are on the margin of society. The man who would serve the community in a region in which farms are being bought and sold should apply his ministry to those who are without land and without capital, because by ministering to them he will serve the whole community. Moreover his service to them should be in the terms of their own life. If he would reach them, he must help them to make money and to use money in helpful and Christian ways.

Example of Wisconsin Minister. A minister in Wisconsin, whose preparation had included some years as detective, to the sharpening of his wits and the increasing of his resources, had become the pastor of a community of railroad men and farmers. Suddenly by the fiat of the railroad, hundreds of his parishioners moved away in a day, leaving the church and the school and the store in a depleted community robbed of more than one half its strength. Mr. Martin turned to the farming of the land himself. Realizing that his parishioners were now only farmers, he led them in the tillage of the soil, setting the example to encourage those who were likely to despair. By his leadership the owners of a pickle factory were induced to build a plant in the community, and farmers were persuaded to undertake the raising of cucumbers on a large scale. He assembled the farmers, and persuaded them, with the storekeeper, to transform the store into a co-operative enterprise, with a capital of $12,000, distributed in one hundred and twenty shares. On this capital interest is paid not to exceed six per cent., and the surplus profit of the store, in which the storekeeper owns ten shares, is distributed equally among the farmers according to the size of their accounts. This community has been re-juvenated by the leadership of a man who was un-willing that a change in the market should ruin the community.

Pastors and Scientific Farming. In the days of organized farming the margin of service is shifted to the farmer who is learning the science of agri-culture. The community leader ministers to these in terms of better farming. By means of improved agriculture they are to survive in the community, and the service to these people on the margin of the community is in training them to till the land by modern science. Such social service as this was demanded by ex-Governor Beaver of Pennsylvania in a public address. " The trouble with the country minister is that he does not know how to farm. The old-style preachers could farm and did farm. They taught their people how to farm the land. The theological seminaries should so train the minister that he would know how to bore a hole in the ground and see whether that spot would do for the planting of a Baldwin apple-tree."

Ministry in Social Terms. Near Albion, New York, in the great apple country, the Rev. Mr. Hares has extended the service of his church to the people of the whole community. Like every other successful act, it is difficult to analyze, but the obvious thing is that the people of the community have been united through a ministry to the young people and the working people. The church is thronged with gatherings at which all are present. The programs of these social meetings are musical, literary, recreative, and they appeal to the mind which in that community is marginal. For the trouble in that great, rich apple country is lack of social life which will make the country worth while. There is plenty of money, but little motive for workingmen or for the youth of the community to remain out in the country where the money is made. The service of this church is founded in a ministry to the whole community in social terms, and its results are gathered in religious union and spiritual gains.

Ministry in Economic Terms. Professor L. H. Bailey of Cornell University says that the best system of coöperative creameries in the United States is in Minnesota, and it was the work of a country minister. Ministers who are so helping the community as this one are able to command the religious forces of the community, because they serve the marginal needs of the community. The Minnesota parish of which this man was minister was suffering from the poverty under which the milk farmer must labor. Under his guidance they were lifted out of this condition and their example has been widely followed throughout the State. Each of these cases serves to illustrate the principle of selection, by which social service shall be successful. That principle is that, to serve the whole community, a man or woman must bestow his life upon those who, being helped, will benefit the whole community.

Duty of Evangelism. True evangelism is an expression of this principle, but much evangelism ignores it. In the open country the village church has the duty of evangelism. The people of the village church cannot have the same influence in the country as country people can have, and their pastor, as a rule, cannot be a pastor of country people if he does not live among them. All the more clearly is his duty as an evangelist seen.

Ministry in Evangelism. The Rev. Clair S. Adams, "the little minister," of Bement, Illinois, has five out-stations from his church in the town. Against the affectionate protest of his people he has gone on a wide circuit for several years past, and has bound up into one great parish a number of school districts, abandoned churches, and neglected fields. The invitations to him for further work of this sort are more than he is able to meet. Mr. Adams is a man of fine evangelistic spirit; while at the same time a sociological student and worker of ripe experience. In his preaching, out in the country, he preaches the conversion of the soul. Frequent revivals attend his ministry, throughout the whole region. His devoted assistant, Miss Bowen, is of the same spirit, and her work has been honored by the courts, in her appointment as probation officer throughout this region. A finer example could not be had of the ministry of a village church, through its workers, to the margin of a great farming community.

Example of Dr. Persons. At Cazenovia, New York, Dr. Silas E. Persons has in the same way yoked up the country districts with his town church. In the town he is a pastor : in the country he is an evangelist. The preaching of a simple gospel of repentance and salvation characterizes the occasional visits to the country, in which he cannot render the elaborate and detailed service of a resident pastor. But in these neglected and remote districts this is precisely the service needed. Dr. Persons is convinced of the great value of evangelism to the people on the outer rim of the town. They are marginal people to the town market, to the social life, and to the churches of the town. To them evangelism is the proper marginal service.

Secret of Sunday's Success. Evangelism, if it be obedient to this principle of social service, must interpret the people on the margin of the community in their own terms. The Rev. " Billy " Sunday is a noted figure in the religious life of the Middle West. His meetings are triumphantly successful in many industrial centers. No one need defend the

CHURCH ERECTED ONE YEAR AGO AT A COST OF $4,000

PREACHING ONCE A MONTH. NO RESIDENT PASTOR IN THE TOWNSHIP

violations of good taste of which he is accused.
My purpose here is to say that his success seems to
be based on his knowledge of the thought and feeling of the working people of the towns. He knows
how to talk their language. He has been a man of
the street, a ball player, and remains still at heart a
marginal man. There is nothing nice or proper
about him. There is everything vigorous, hearty,
and zealous. The result is that his meetings are
thronged with the very people who live on the margin of these communities. Working men without
capital, laborers who do not own their tools, renters
who do not own the land they till, all come to
his meetings. The striking thing is that, while his
violence of language frequently offends the well-to-
do people of the community, he always attracts
them to the meetings before the series is over. Conspicuous among his most thorough converts are people who are central to the life of the community,
lawyers, delicate women, owners of large business
plants, and occasionally he makes a convert of an
exquisite preacher.

A Young College Graduate's Achievement. In
the middle of Illinois there is a farming community,
centering in a hamlet, where for thirty years there
had been no religious service. A student graduating
from college spent the summer on his father's farm
and began to hold meetings assisted by the young
people of his church, in this neglected neighborhood, which was the common margin of three or
four surrounding towns. His work was attended

with extraordinary results, and within a year a chapel was erected, comfortable and ample for the seating of two hundred people, and the gratitude of the neighborhood was expressed in a stained-glass window, in which they insisted on placing his name. They call it the Lin Hurie Chapel. His work had the extraordinary value that religious service has to the margin of community life.

The Ministry of a Gentle Woman. In 1907 the Committee on Morals and Rural Conditions, of the Congregational Conference of Massachusetts, whose duties were to evangelize as well as to study the neglected regions lying between the towns of certain portions of the State, requested the appointment of a woman for this work. Miss Anna B. Taft had that year attended the Silver Bay Conference of the Missionary Education Movement and had been inspired with a desire to serve in some definite capacity for the people near her home. She was employed for this work, and entered upon two years of devoted service, with constantly increasing influence, to the marginal people of Massachusetts. Her growing influence and usefulness were due, not merely to her gentle breeding and capacity for abundance of work, but in part to the exceptional value of her religious ministry to marginal people.

"Brush Arbor" Churches. In Tennessee, Kentucky, Missouri, and other States of the Southwest, churches are very often founded as "brush arbor" churches, a meeting being appointed in a neighborhood where there is no "church-house." The

" brush arbor " is made in a grove of trees.   Fastening rude timbers overhead from tree to tree, and driving poles in the ground, where necessary for a support, a roof is made by rudely thatching the area with boughs cut from trees.   Thus the people are protected from the sun and in some degree from rain.   These " brush arbor " churches will seat five hundred people on occasion.   The seats are made, as the other furniture, by driving stakes in the ground for the support of planks on which the people sit.   It is said by superintendents of churches in this section that many of the best churches in the Southwest grew out of " brush arbor " beginnings. This is a method which explores the margin of religious organization and is eminently well suited to the open country and the temperate climate of the southwestern States.

Enterprising Village Blacksmith.   At Florida, New York, the old church of the farmers is matched now by a church of Roman Catholic Poles.   The old Protestant folk are slowly losing ground: the Poles are rapidly gaining.   The Poles are industrious, thrifty, and far-sighted in their farming. The Presbyterians are inclined to abandon the farm for the life of the cities, but in the old church is a brotherhood of men who under the leadership of the town blacksmith, a man who has had the same shop in the village for over fifty years, have undertaken community enterprises.   The success in these enterprises is due to the fact that they serve marginal needs of the community.

Streets Lighted and Bank Organized. The first move was to light the streets of the town. Much discomfort and some disorder had resulted from dark streets. The whole village united in the enterprise of lighting it, and has shared the common benefit. The second enterprise formed by this brotherhood was the floating of a bank in the village. The saloonkeeper had been the banker, and the working men of the town had been obliged to pay him a heavy tax for the cashing of checks. When the men of the Presbyterian church proposed a bank they got the allegiance for the first time of the Polish Catholics, who voted solidly, with their priest at their head, in favor of the bank at the popular meeting called by the brotherhood. Both these enterprises were on the margin of the town's needs. These older citizens studied the community as a whole, and served all by supplying those needs which were most felt by the working people and the young people of the town.

Immigrants are Marginal People. The immigrant is marginal to American communities. Whatever is done for him, since he helps the community to earn their living, will benefit the whole community. He has come to stay. His life is big with future possibilities. They who would minister to the whole community must minister to him. This subject is itself great enough for a volume, but I will indicate briefly the forms of ministry to the immigrant which are adapted to his marginal needs.

A Welcome to Italians. It should be a service of Americans to foreigners. Important as the foreign speech is, the most important thing of all is the American welcome. Therefore, whatever is done must be done in American courtesy to newcomers from abroad. This spirit is finely expressed in the celebration of the Italian national holiday by a Pennsylvania town. Around Grove City is a large Italian population of miners. At dawn of the national holiday of Italy, August 8th, the town was awakened by the playing of a band and tumultuous explosion of fireworks. Thus began the long day of music, games, and illumination. By invitation of the President of Grove City College, Dr. Isaac C. Ketler, these foreigners used for the day, with great respect, affection, and self-restraint, the college campus, the most beautiful park in the neighborhood. This illustrates the principle. These men will always feel welcome, and will find themselves at home in the community in which the leading citizens have given them such a welcome.

Teaching Aliens English. The language of the country should be taught to the foreigner. The Young Men's Christian Association does this successfully, and the book by Dr. Peter Roberts is to be commended as a quick and valuable method of " Teaching English to Foreigners."

Evangelization of Foreigners. The evangelization of foreigners, when they have been welcomed and taught the English language, has great possibilities. This is a Christian land to them. They easily learn, if there be those to teach them, that religion means something nobler and finer in a free country than they have known it in a government of compulsion. The swift growth in the number of Italian churches throughout the country is sufficient evidence. In fifteen years they have increased from five to over three hundred, and the most of these have come into existence in the last five years of the fifteen. The success of this work is due to the fact that the foreigner is generally a marginal man, to whom Protestant Christianity has extraordinary value. No greater service can be rendered by Protestant churches to future generations than to Americanize the foreigners and lead them to Christ.

Variety of Activities. Social service must, therefore, understand the modes of life of the people who are on the edge of the community. It must be sympathetic with children, with adolescents, with working men, and with " renters." For this reason recreation is a great element in marginal service, because recreation has the value for working men that higher education has for the well-to-do. Industrial education is a principle of marginal service, because training in getting a living is a big factor in the life of working people. But the important thing is the principle of selection, which guided the Master himself, the principle, namely, that to serve the whole community one must minister to the people who are in jeopardy, and enable those to stand who are likely to fall. One must find the lost and restore them. He must heal the sick. Thus he will

play upon the heart-strings of the community. He
will command the social instinct. He will turn on
the currents of electric sympathies which will become his resources, and on his side will be the whole
power of social organization which controls the
every-day action of all the people of the whole
community.

LEADERSHIP OF THE COMMUNITY

Any consideration of the problem of rural life that leaves out of account the function and the possibilities of the Church, and of related institutions, would be grossly inadequate.

This is not because in the last analysis the country-life problem is a moral problem, or that in the best development of the individual the great motives and results are religious and spiritual, but because from the pure sociological point of view the Church is fundamentally a necessary institution in country life. In a peculiar way the Church is intimately related to the agricultural industry. The work and the life of the farm are closely bound together, and the institutions of the country react on that life and on one another more intimately than they do in the city. This gives the rural Church a position of peculiar difficulty and one of unequaled opportunity. The time has arrived when the Church must take a larger leadership, both as an institution and through its pastors, in the social reorganization of rural life.

The great spiritual needs of the country community just at present are higher personal and community ideals. Rural people need to have an aspiration for the highest possible development of the community. There must be an ambition on the part of the people themselves constantly to progress in all of those things that make the community life wholesome, satisfying, educative, and complete. There must be a desire to develop a permanent environment for the country boy and girl of which they will become passionately fond. As a pure matter of education, the countryman must learn to love the country and to have an intellectual appreciation of it. More than this, the spiritual nature of the individual must be kept thoroughly alive. His personal ideals of conduct and ambition must be cultivated.

Of course the Church has an indispensable function as a conservator of morals. But from the social point of view, it is to hold aloft the torch of personal and community idealism. It must be a leader in the attempt to idealize country life.—*Report of the Country Life Commission*

VIII

LEADERSHIP OF THE COMMUNITY

Reasons for Lack of Leadership. There are reasons for lack of leadership in the community. The first of these is the leveling of the country population by the sifting out of all modes of getting a living except farming. Country people tend to be reduced to one economic experience. It is true that in only a few communities has this process been completed, but in all the effect of it is apparent in the growing consciousness of farm work rather than social life. The thought of farm people about their own life is purely industrial. It is a thought of work rather than of association, and the work is agriculture.

Strange Interpretation of Democracy. It is characteristic of working people and farmers that they interpret democracy in terms of level and uniform equality. Farmers especially are loath to admit that there are any leaders in their community. One of the most puzzling obstacles in the way of a country minister is the assent of all his people to the proposition " We have no leaders here." It is a theory they have about democracy that the ideal condition is one of equality in which no man stands out as

greater than his neighbor.   It is the " make-believe "
by which they play the game of life.

No Common Socializing Experience.   A deeper
cause of this condition is the lack of socializing experience in the country.   Rural communities are con-
trasted to urban or town communities by going
through the round of the year without any notable
event or celebration unless they assemble in the
town or village.   A community made up of working
farmers generally celebrates no anniversary, and
keeps no great holiday.   This is a very curious nega-
tion, especially for American people; but in a country community the Fourth of July awakens no local
spirit, Thanksgiving brings no grateful response,
Christmas day is celebrated, if at all, in the household alone, and Easter is not regularly a great day
in the church.   Of course there are exceptions.   I
am describing only the prevailing condition.   In the
absence of customary meetings of the countryside,
it is natural that leadership should not be evolved.
The community itself, that is to say, the people who
live within a convenient team-haul of one another,
do not have those accustomed contacts that would
distinguish one above another.   If there is a meeting in the course of the year to which all the families are attracted, it is probably in a town, and it
generally exploits the country community while con-
tributing nothing to it.   The circus in a near-by city
is attended by every one.   The county fair at the
county seat is very popular.   Such as these are annual events on which all attend, but their influence

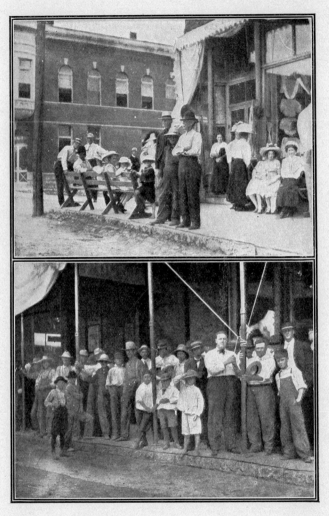

SATURDAY AFTERNOON IN TOWN

is to drain and to weaken rather than to enrich and distinguish the country community.

No Natural Meeting-places. It is very strange, too, that with the closing of the old country stores away from the railroad, the country community has lost its only places of informal meeting. The men of the community have no natural meeting-places. Their leisure is not attracted by any magnet within the community. The women may be somewhat more fortunate, for their church connections take the form of sewing circles and Ladies' Aid societies, but the men and boys are by their work drawn apart from one another. Their sport and recreation, so far as the community goes, is solitary. Hunting or fishing does not tend to produce leadership but rather to undermine it. There can be no persons known to a whole population except through continued leisurely and voluntary association. Out of such mingling, dependent not on compulsion, but on free and ingenuous life together, leadership is developed. Whatever common experiences there are in the course of the year will give character to the leaders who exist in the community. At the places of informal association these gatherings with the men who there assemble will continue to describe the leaders who stand before the community as a whole.

Results of Surveys in Pennsylvania and Illinois. The Surveys made by the Department of Church and Country Life in Pennsylvania and in Illinois in 1909 showed a surprising tendency of country communities to be unprogressive. In fifty communities there were found only two conspicuous individuals who were acknowledged by the farmers about them to be leaders. Neither of these individuals is a farmer. No community was found in which the farmers would acknowledge that a farmer was a leader among them. The two leaders in these fifty communities were, one of them a schoolmaster, one of them an old soldier and politician.

Leadership is Denied. Under these conditions individual life withers as leadership is denied. The man who attempts to live as the equal of all other men will coöperate with none, for coöperation means subjection. His ideal of a man, to which he conforms his actions, is that of an independent personality, owning land, paying his debts, and " caring for nobody." This is not the highest ideal of a human being. I do not say that it is universal among farmers, but I believe it is the ideal which prevails among those populations in which the sifting process is removing from the farm all other modes of getting a living except farming.

The Residue Degenerate. The tendency of this ideal is toward degeneracy on the part of many, brilliancy on the part of a few, and discouragement among the greater number. Those communities which assent to this ideal of personality, which deny leadership and refuse to allow distinction among their own number, shortly lose the more brilliant members of the community. Boys and girls who are restless for distinction and aim at leadership

WILD ANIMAL SHOW

SAFE AND SANE FOURTH OF JULY IN THE OPEN COUNTRY

leave the community and go off to school or to the city, and find there a truer expression of their own ideas. Those who cannot go, because they cannot sell their land, remain in the community, their men have a vote, and the members of their families " are as good as anybody." The result in their case is degeneration. They cannot live the same life as the average persons in the community. They tend to a lower level and their failure to maintain their position is discouraging. In the case of some members of these families, the result is insanity and suicide. One cause of this condition seems to be the inability of these people to maintain the ideal to which they and their fathers assented, that is, a respectable equality with all other men, especially with all in their community. To fall behind in the race seems to them intolerable.

Church Should Develop Leadership. The duty of the country Church, therefore, is to utilize the occasions which make leaders. These occasions arise in the regular meetings of the whole population. For this purpose Sunday preaching services are most influential, but are not sufficient, because the Sunday preaching service is itself based on the wrong ideal when it is made the only means to these ends. It presumes that all men are alike. The Church should provide an annual gathering of the whole population.

Jamesburg Anniversary. One church, in Jamesburg, New Jersey, which has such a meeting, calls it " The Anniversary." Nobody knows what it commemorates. Its origin is forgotten, but its value throughout the years is very great. It fills a large place in the community life. It brings home once a year the older members of the community. It arouses local pride in the success of every son of the community who has done well. It stimulates the aspirations of the young, and above all, it warms up the isolation of the individual with a sense of belonging to a distinguished company.

Reunions and Old Home Week. An old church in Wassaic, Dutchess County, New York, had a recent reunion, to which a visit or a letter was secured from every living son of the community. It gave to the members of a discouraged country church and to the remainders of families living in the countryside a sense of distinction, of being a part of the great world, which they had not had before. The Old Home Week in New England is a fine expression of this annual meeting of the community. It is of special value for the older places which have a departed population. It calls them home or brings from them a letter or a contribution. It marks the historic places in the community with some memorial in granite or in bronze. It brings distinguished speakers to a great open-air gathering and it seats the whole countryside together at the table.

Religious Festivals. But above all, the country community should celebrate the great holidays of the year. Charles Kingsley has a fine passage on the value of the Church year to the Church of England congregations. It brings before them all the round of human experience. In America the celebrations of the country community should not be those of European saints, but should be the anniversaries of American sentiment and experience. The Church year should begin with a gathering at Christmas time in celebration of the Lord's birth. Gifts made by the whole community to the children, in which no child should be omitted, no matter what his religious belief, can at this time bring all together. The writer remembers with tenderness and gratitude the day when as a child he first recited a few verses in a Christmas dialogue on the church platform. It was a profound and lasting religious experience. At this time, also, the celebration can take the form of song.

Christmas Appeal Universal. Choruses, cantatas, or even in some communities an oratorio, are possible at Christmas which would be unattainable at any other time. It is the season of the year at which country people have the most leisure. The rehearsals may be made occasions of the highest social value, but above all, the Christmas celebration should be of such a character that none shall be left out. Neither the Catholic nor the Jew, if they be present in the community, should be excluded. There is something about the Christmas celebration which appeals to all mankind. It must be made a time for enlarging the countryman's idea of himself. By the play of sentiment the individual man must have his eyes opened beyond the horizon of his own farm and his own family to the whole community and the whole human family.

Easter and Immortality.   Similarly the celebration of Easter is favorable for the development of religious leadership.   Country people generally believe in the resurrection and in immortality.   The country minister who is adequate to the religious leadership of his people ought to know how to coin this universal belief in immortality into a great celebration at Easter time.   Printed aids are furnished with some fulness by religious agencies, but it is far better to depend upon local possibilities and to develop the day in song, in the decoration of the church, and in the general celebration of the season itself in such way as to minister religiously to the community.

Easter and Evangelism.   It seems to the writer that the Easter season is the best time for evangelism. The approach of this sacred day, whose tradition enters so deeply into the belief in immortality, should be made holy.   Amusement, recreation, and ordinary social life should be discouraged, and the fruitage of the whole year in religious sentiment should be harvested through individual expressions.   Immortality is at the opposite pole from social feeling. Our hopes of immortal life are personal.   Therefore at Easter time the preacher should devote himself to the development of the individuals among his people.   Conversion should at this time result from the general work throughout the year.

Community's Objective Determines Type of Leader.   The essential thing is the spirit of developing the community's own life in its own terms.   The

value of all this will show itself in the rise of leaders among the people themselves. As before indicated, the leadership will be of like character with
the means by which that leadership is produced. If
the means be religious, ethical, and social, the leaders who shall arise will be devout, moral, and popular men. If the meetings of the people are purely
for business purposes, the leaders of the town will
be concerned alone with its business prosperity. It
is the business of the minister and the teacher in the
country community so to agitate the community and
so to unite it that the leaders of the community
shall be men of conscience, of intelligence, and of a
progressive spirit. If the loafers of the town are the
only ones who have opportunity for frequent association, then the loafers will select the leaders. But
if the regular meetings of the town are bright, intellectual, and popular; if the enjoyment is furnished
by music, by dramatic expression, by the remem-
brance of the past of the community, and by planning for the future, then the leadership of the
town will flow from these sources, and the common
mind of the community will demand and will secure
those personalities who shall stand before all the
people to accomplish that for which the whole people
aspire.

Revivals and Leadership. Evangelism creates
leaders. Men's souls are saved that they may become priests and prophets of God. All the means
described above for the cultivation of leaders have
been practised by ministers in the country, but are

dependent upon the discovery of devoted men and women through their thorough conversion and re-generation. If the community has a few who give their lives for the Kingdom, it may train them in these ways for larger service. But above all, the annual pilgrimage to the valley of decision must bring men's souls before God. Persuade those whose heart God has touched to confess their faith in him. The best times for this revival of religion are in the late fall and the early spring. Communities differ in this, but some period is especially suitable, and at this time the great and holy day of decision should be made the first of all holidays. Every energy of the Church should be turned toward the conversion of souls.

All Organizations Have Symbols. All societies are united under some kind of a symbol. Armies march behind banners, and because their organization is artificial and intense, they have numerous standards, guides, and emblems. But natural societies cannot get on without the same service. People rally very often around a symbol which serves the mere purpose of assembling them, with more enthusiasm than for the purposes of their common life. Men will sometimes do more for the flag than they will do for what the flag represents. Nevertheless, the flag serves a purpose in uniting them, and this is itself of great value.

Community Symbol is the Church. The country community, like every other society, is united in a symbol, and in the country this symbol is the church. The spire rising above the trees, by the roadside, serves as a pivot of rural interest. The weekly meeting has varying meanings, with the change of ministers and with the variation of their themes, but it has an unchanging value for the community as a place to assemble and as a token that the people are one.

Worship is for Everybody. The flag of the country community is the church. This is the common center around which all may rally. Its doctrines and its membership are for a limited number, but its worship is for everybody. The sound of its bell comes to all hearts, and the influence of its uniting power is upon the whole countryside. The old-time ministers were statesmen and they held their churches up against the whole community. We have too frequently forgotten this meaning of the church, as a token of the people's common life. It is none the less real, and it can be restored.

Likeness Attracts Individuals. Consciousness of kind is recognized by sociologists as an organizing force. Those who respond to common stimuli become aware of their resemblances and their differences. They recognize a certain oneness, and immediately a society is born. It may be a great one or a small one, but the foundations of societies are laid when men become aware that they are like unto one another and different from the rest.

Doak Organized Differing Communities. When Samuel Doak, a graduate of Princeton College, came on horseback through East Tennessee to Nola

Chucky River, he stopped in the woods to inquire the way, of men who were chopping. They learned that he was a minister, and asked him to preach. So sitting on his horse as he was, he preached a sermon to the assembled pioneers. They gathered about him and constrained him to remain as their pastor. This was about 1795. He began his ministry, and at the same time laid the foundations of Washington College, the earliest college to be founded west of the Alleghanies. For a few years his people were conscious of their kinship to Dr. Doak. But shortly a sense of difference arose, and he felt constrained to go further and unite himself with the people of Tusculum, fifteen miles southwestward, where he again built up a country community and where again he founded a college, which became Tusculum College. These two communities were organized as churches. The church was the symbol of the community's life. These churches still remain, each intensely conscious of its kinship to the people in its own community, and having a sense of difference from the people in the other community founded by Samuel Doak. So intense was this consciousness of difference that when the pioneer preacher died, and they carried his body to be buried at Washington College, it is said that very few of the first settlers came out to pay respect to his remains.

Churches Recognize Social Divisions. Worship is the truest expression we have of conciousness of kind. In America, where there are no state

churches, the worship of God is the freest common
function in which all the people are represented.
It expresses, therefore, with infallible accuracy, the
consciousness of differences and of resemblances in
the mind of the people. For in the hurried and
changing reorganization of recent years the churches
have harbored the social feelings of the people. We
have come to have " rich men's churches," " working men's churches," " student pastors," " sailors'
Bethels," " slum chapels," and other Church organizations which are symbols of the social divisions
in which the people live.

Color Causes Divisions. The most striking expression of consciousness of kind, as reflected in the
Church, is in the South. Before the war the Negroes
worshiped with their masters, but when they were
freed by the Emancipation Proclamation, they went
out to build their own churches and the South has
to-day churches for the white, and churches for the
Negro, in all its States. The fact that this division
represents the feelings of all the people of the South
is evidenced by this, that the Negro churches are
very largely erected with the white man's money.
The black trace their consciousness of kinship in
accordance with color and racial history by the
worship of the Lord's Day.

**Church Must Recognize Fundamental Social
Feelings.** There is, of course, much to be lamented
in this social division of the people. I am anxious
here only to trace it and to recognize clearly the
place which worship has in social organization.

We will not be able to build the community Church, unless we recognize clearly the principle by which churches serve the people, in expressing fundamental social feelings. The Church is the symbol of the social life of the whole people.

Minister Must Know Community's Sentiments. The minister's need of social knowledge is most evident at this point. Unless he knows how the people feel, and makes himself the expression of that feeling, he cannot lead them. For instance, in New England the proprieties require that a man's sins be not discussed at his funeral. No matter how bad he may have been, the community does not need to be told of it on that occasion. It is a part of the decorum rooted in the feelings of all New England people that the dead should be decently laid away, and that something be said appropriate to the occasion. I remember the comment of two typical Yankees, made in reference to the funeral addresses by pastors over departed friends. In either case the man who died had his faults, and in both cases the minister had seen fit to deal familiarly with these faults. In so doing he had put himself out of sympathy with the community. He lost his power to act for them all, and weakened his influence.

Pastor Who Unites Community. Some farming communities have expressed themselves so perfectly in the life of the minister, and he has represented with such precision their common life, that his days have been passed, even down to old age, with them. The Rev. J. L. Braddock came to the church at Winnebago, Illinois, at forty-eight years of age. The end of his pastorate came in his ninety-first year. Forty-two years he represented that community, and so intimate was the sympathy between him and them, so truly did he use the symbol of the community, that the whole population at the end of his pastorate was represented in its membership, save two or three families; and the streams of life of the households, the children, the young people, the women, and the men in their respective organizations flowed through that church. Such an instance expresses the satisfaction of the community in the church and its leader.

A Woman Unites Divergent Classes. I have known a woman to embody the life of the community. She was endowed with rare and intense social sympathy. Magnetic in personality and possessed of ample means, she compelled the allegiance of all. Those whom she united in one experience of community feeling were divergent from one another in the widest degrees. The very old and the very young, the very rich and proud, the very poor and discouraged, found in her an experience of sympathy with their condition, and through her, sympathized with one another. For fifteen years her life was theirs, and their needs were her daily thought. But the medium of this influence was the country church, in which she was a member, which they all attended. The various organizations in this country church touched the lives of all the people in the community, and in all these organizations her influence was felt.

Illinois Example. In an Illinois town, in which I am deeply interested, the country church, out in the open fields, has been the center of great interest. The schools have been consolidated alongside the church. The holidays of the year are celebrated under the leadership of the church people. A nearby abandoned neighborhood in which there has been no preaching for many years has been annexed to the parish, and the whole community is united in one house of worship. Yet in this community the most influential men deny that they are leaders. They recognize that in order to lead they must appear to follow. There is no country squire among them. They instinctively feel that if any man took on the airs of leadership, he would at once lose all his followers. For such a situation the country Church is the available symbol, which furnishes a medium of exchange of influences. It embodies the unity of the countryside under cover of which all these things can be done by a few families, indeed, very often by just one household in which is possessed the power of leadership. The standard which all follow is held high, but the standard-bearer is not seen.

Magnify the Church in the Community. If the Church is the symbol of the community, it follows that to train people in community ways one must magnify the Church. There is needed to-day a great Protestant movement for reinterpreting religious life in terms of the Church. It must be broad-minded and tolerant in the truest sense, but nevertheless it will be an organizing of Christian sentiment and a reassembling of Christian people in congregations which serve communities. If we ever come to have the country organized in communities and the life of individuals inspiring the deeds in their communities, we will inevitably have the Church as the token of the community's oneness, standing out in the open country with its people about it.

Weakness in Individualism. The evident weakness of the present-day Protestant sentiment is its individualism. Solitary living has given us a solitary religion. We have been ruled by pioneer men and pioneer standards, but pioneer days are gone forever. Our evangelism has been content to tell salvation to the individual soul and lay no bondage upon that soul for service to the community. We have worked in our churches and Sunday-schools for the regeneration of the youth and have had nothing for them of a regenerate sort when it was done. The result is that the Sunday-school terminates its influence over most of the children at about fifteen years of age. But ideals are needed to take up the life of our young people or of those converted and harness them to the great task of the world.

Foreign Mission Ideal. Within the past twenty years the foreign mission propaganda has furnished such an ideal and has possessed the minds of the young men and women in the schools and colleges. It expresses itself in the formula " Religion means

God, myself, and the world." We must have a new ideal more intensive than this and nearer home. For the most of men cannot lay their soul under bondage to the whole world. The Christian man can live in his community, but not one in a hundred is capable of practising the "world idea," and if the "world idea" is to be of influence among the home-dwelling folk, it must come to them through the distributing center of a community institution. The country Church is necessary for sustaining the great project of evangelizing the world.

Church Should Dominate Individual and Community. Christian sentiment must be reshaped and Christian people must be reënlisted in the interest of the Church as a specific expression of the kingdom of God. We need change no vital principle of the Protestant heritage. We have been unfaithful to this heritage in our diffuse and diluted individualism. We need stern, vigorous reorganization of life, which will express itself in churches so strong as to dominate the individual life and so extensively organized as to penetrate the whole community with their influence.

Saved to Serve. The trouble we have to overcome is a weak, good-natured conception that the Christian is saved by certain emotional experiences he has had, and the Church is no more business of his. He is to live a good life and avoid scandal, and when necessary he is to be waited on by Church organizations, sustained by other people, and held together by those who are more narrow and more

traditional in their type than he.   But the strong
personalities of the world, the literary minds, the
persons who love nature and " can worship in the
woods," the esthetic souls who need the means of
culture, these conceive that having received the message of salvation which the Church has to give them,
they have done all that is taught in Christianity and
owe no further duty.   For this state of mind the
traditional evangelism and the customary preaching
are to blame.   Individual souls have been over-
dosed with a gospel of their personal importance.
Protestantism has become centrifugal.   It has been
diluted with a false idealism.   There is no organizing principle in very much of it, and a great deal of
the individualism of our time, the selfish culture of
learned men, the masterful independence and ruth-
less loneliness of some rich men, have been extreme
results of this false idealism.   Though they are extreme results, they are logical and inevitable.   We
cannot preach an unmodified doctrine of personal
salvation without having these results.

Enlist for Community Betterment.   The needed
teaching in our time is that of the organized community.   Christian people and other well-meaning
folk must all assemble as the leaders and must be
enlisted as the workers in community betterment.
They must be taught to recognize clearly the bounds
of their community.   They must come to see how
fully their own lives and the lives of their children
and kindred are spent in that little environment.
They must make of it a republic to be ruled in

sanitary respects, in all matters of beauty and in the recreative life, in the interest of developing personality and of the unfolding social life. In the service of this little republic to the influence of the Church will be the dominating element. If Christian churches are not the community centers, then new churches will arise. This great task will be done.

Denmark's Example. The progress of the country life movement in Denmark illustrates this tendency of community organization to build churches. The Church has been organized and new structures have been erected wherever the people have been assembled in working and serviceable units. They have needed a symbol of their oneness. Although the regeneration of Denmark was carried on by the schoolmasters, who wrought out its details and bore the burden of its routine, both the beginning and the ending of it were the work of ministers of religion. It was inspired by Bishop Grundtvig and his associates; and when it was matured it expressed itself in church building and church organization. The seed of it and the flower of it were religious, but the stalk and stem and branch were educational.

Devotion to Community. Therefore the sum of the whole matter is this. The Christian man or woman in America, especially in the open country, must learn to devote himself to the community, and to this end must magnify the Church as the community center. A new formula will control his life. He shall say, " Religion consists, for me, of God in the community, and in the world." This cannot be done without magnifying the Church, but attention must not be first of all upon the Church. A selfish Church that seeks the obedience of men and demands their craven submission cannot do this work, but the Church which preaches the gospel of common service in a common local task, and offers its own house and its own walls and its own minister for this use will build itself and will be enlarged in the process of serving the community.

Rural Life Out of Repair. To review, therefore: country life is out of repair. Rural institutions have been breaking down under the influences of speculation in land. The causes of this dilapidation of social life in the country are transitional. They will soon pass away. Religious people are all summoned, therefore, to provide for the new day of organized farming which is to come. It is for them to idealize it, and to express its spirit in a new conception of life. This conception of life is to be expressed in the Church, the center of the community.

Four Phases and Types. Country life has passed through three or four phases leading to maturity. Each of these phases has been under the domination of a new type of men; the solitary farmer, the household farmer, the speculative farmer, and the organized farmer. Each of these has built his own community, centering it in a church of his own sort. These churches and communities have been so unlike one another that what is thought good in the one is thought wrong in the other. In the eyes of the pioneer the warm social ways of the household farmer are sinful. Yet these successive stages of community life are cumulative. All that was good in the earlier stage is retained until the later ones, and in the day of organized farming, which is dawning, the methods and even the personalities of pioneer, of household, and of speculative farming will have their place.

Central Place of the Church. The task of organizing the Church to respond to the scientific agriculture of our day is exceedingly intricate. It will be a highly organized and sympathetic institution. It can be no less than the center of the whole community. It cannot afford that any part of the community be outside its influence. For this reason modern Christian people are craving the federation of the churches in order that the Church may truly reflect the life of a coöperating and uniting people.

Reorganized Country Schools. The schools in the country need to be reorganized to serve the needs of Christian communities. The principle of this reconstruction is the teaching of science to the farmer as a preparation for country life. Not merely to make the farmer rich is the motive in the new schools in the country, but while enriching him to win him to a new rural idealism and to make of him a new type of countryman. This is the principle on which the schools in the country must be rebuilt. For this purpose the centralizing and consolidating of the common schools is necessary. Not in all places, for there will remain many one-room country schools which serve their purpose in the corners of the land. But the system of schools in the country must be reorganized on the radius of the team-haul; the children assembled in large groups for social intercourse, and for constructive moral and spiritual culture.

Spirit of Coöperation. Farming is essentially coöperative. Those farmers have survived through the recent period of change who inherited from their ancestors the practise of coöperation, and they alone have survived. The uncoöperative farming which prevailed throughout the country has suffered severely under the influence of speculation in land. The home, the Church, and the school in the country, where unprotected by coöperation, have been undermined by the speculative process of the past twenty years. The growth of coöperative customs among farmers is, therefore, to be encouraged by the churches for self-protection and for building up country communities immune to the changes in the value of land or of farm products. Country life will come into possession of itself only through federation of the farmers in their own interest.

Federation of Churches. This coöperation in economic life is the true preparation for the federation of the churches. The material and other relations of life must all become organic and one before the symbols of the people's life which are in the churches reorganize. The Heavenly Father is at work among the people, feeding, clothing, enriching, and organizing them, and he cares more for the welfare of the people than for the survival of the churches. He is shepherd of the flock, and if he must change the fold, he will not forget his care of the sheep. Wherever the flock is reassembled it will be easy to build a new fold. Wherever the people are coöperative in their life and organize in communities, the federation of churches will surely follow.

Pauperism Abolished. The new prosperity which has come in the country must be trained by community organization, first of all, to care for the poor. Pauperism must be excluded from the community. It is impossible to have any real prosperity while any number in the neighborhood is in want. It is impossible for intelligence to be real and for culture to be genuine while ignorance and destitution are near at hand. The country community must be made the clearing-house for the protection and the sustaining of those who are without land and without productive tools. Moreover, we are learning new methods of distributing the wealth of the people in the interest of the whole people, and these methods are religious. They are already a part of the work of the churches. It is important for religious people to use the democratic methods, born of their own necessities, by the transformation of pew-renting and other older customs into the democratic support of the church by small regular contributions from all. The vital character of the churches is shown in this struggle for democracy in giving.

Ministry to Marginal People. The principle of social service is the care of the poor. During our lifetime there will be men without land and without tools in America and probably in increasing proportions. While we are discussing the far-distant future when poverty is to be abolished, it becomes us to take measures for its repression now in the country community, where pauperism can be abolished. The principle of social service is the ministry of those who have means and leadership to the people on the edge of the community, to those who are in jeopardy, and whose hold upon social life is constantly in danger. To serve them is to serve all. This is the principle of selection, by which social service shall be rendered with ease and with power.

Church Community Symbol. Finally there is no symbol of all this spirit save the Church. If the people prosper, it will show itself in the Church. If the people are mean, the Church will infallibly represent their sordid spirit. If the people are democratic, the Church will be large-minded. If the people are narrow, their churches will write upon the sky the story of their bigotry. The Church is, therefore, the emblem of the social life of the people. It should be understood as a means of knowing social conditions. It is the sensitive register which they who work for the welfare of mankind may use. The Church is the vehicle of ministry unto all the community. Its power to inspire and to see is beyond the power of any other institution.

Ministry to Common People. For in the life of the whole people dwells the life of the Almighty Father. He cares for them and moves upon them and leads them on through the years of history to his own destined ends. They who are poor and whose welfare depends upon the life of the people as a whole believe in God. Among them there is no doubt, and he who would meet with God must meet him in the life of common folk, who depend for their welfare and for the expression of their faith upon the Church at the center of the community.

QUESTIONS AND REFERENCES

SUGGESTIONS FOR USING THE QUESTIONS

The questions below have been prepared to suggest a few lines of discussion that may be pursued by the average leader of a study class. It must be evident to all that no set of questions can be prepared that will satisfy all leaders. Both the caliber of the leader and the character of the group will vary in every local church. Even persons who have had extensive experience in leading classes will probably find these questions suggestive, and it is hoped that those who are just beginning will receive much help. Few fact questions have been included because they can be easily supplied by any leader from the paragraph headings.

Questions marked with the asterisk (*) should arouse more than ordinary thought and discussion.

QUESTIONS ON CHAPTER I

AIM: To Understand the Principal Causes of Rural Deterioration

1. If you are living in an urban community, in what respects are you dependent upon the agricultural communities?
2.* Is the prosperity of agriculture vital to the prosperity of the nation? Give reasons.
3.* Do you believe that the prosperity of the farmers is of greater importance than the prosperity of the industrial enterprises? State reasons.
4. Why have so many young people gone from the farm to the towns and cities?
5. Do you believe they have really benefited themselves by the change, and in what respects?
6. Describe the four types of rural life in the United States.
7. Which type is the most evident in our country to-day?
8. What do you consider the strength and weakness of each type?
9. Which do you consider the best type in the past, and why?

10. Would you wish to restore that type if it were possible?

11. Which section of the United States is deteriorating most, and why?

12. Which of the phases of rural deterioration is the most disastrous?

13.* Is soil exhaustion a greater menace to agricultural welfare than speculation?

14.* Do you think the fundamental cause for rural decay is economic, social, or religious?

15. Sum up the principal causes of rural deterioration in the order of their importance.

16.* What assistance can people in towns and cities give toward the upbuilding of the rural community?

17. What can scientific farming do to improve conditions?

18. What can the rural inhabitants do to improve conditions?

19.* What can the churches do to improve country life?

REFERENCES FOR ADVANCED STUDY

CHAPTER I

Anderson, The Country Town. I, III, V-IX.

Ashenhurst, The Day of the Country Church, XII.

Bailey, The Country Life Movement, 14-43.

Beard, The Story of John Frederic Oberlin, II, III.

Butterfield, Chapters in Rural Progress, I.

Butterfield, The Country Church and the Rural Problem, I.

Hartt, "The Regeneration of Rural New England," The Outlook, March 3, 10, 17, 31, 1900.

Hyde, "Impending Paganism in New England," The Forum, June, 1892.

Plunkett, The Rural Life Problem in the United States, III. IV.

Roads, Rural Christendom, III.

Strong, The Challenge of the City, I.

Strong, The New Era, VIII.

QUESTIONS ON CHAPTER II

AIM: TO SHOW THE INTIMATE RELATION OF THE CHURCH TO THE COMMUNITY

1. Have you ever seen a prosperous agricultural community without a church?

2. Do you think people in the country are more religious than those in towns and cities?

3.* Has the man who is in touch with the forces of nature any advantages in strengthening his religious faith over the dweller in town and city?

4. Can the minister in a rural parish relate people to God more intimately than the minister in a city?

5.* Are the people in a rural community more accessible to the minister than those in a town or city?

6. What do you consider the best definition of a country community?

7.* Compare the Church as an organizing center in a community with any other organization in the rural community.

8. What do you consider some of the defects of the individualist Church?

9. Has emotion any legitimate place in the religious life?

10. Will communities be saved as groups or as individuals?

11. What were some of the limitations of the household Church?

12.* What features in the household Church would you wish to conserve?

13. What are the advantages and disadvantages of the competitive system in religious life?

14. If you were a minister in a household farming community, what would be the burden of your message to the people?

15.* Enumerate the evil effects of speculation upon the Church.

16.* What recommendations for effective service would you make to a minister working in a community where the spirit of speculation is abroad?

17.* What can a minister do to get the people in a modern farming community to make the Church more helpful to the people?

18. Is it easier for people to coöperate in agriculture than in religion?

19. What can the Church do to minister to the social and economic needs of all the people?

20. Should the Church direct its main efforts upon winning and training the young people or adults in a community. Give reasons.

21. Has the Church in a rural community an opportunity to do more for people than one located in an urban community?

REFERENCES FOR ADVANCED STUDY

CHAPTER II

Anderson, The Country Town, XVI.

Ashenhurst, The Day of the Country Church, I-III.

Beard, The Story of John Frederic Oberlin, III.

Boyle, "The Passing of the Country Church," The Outlook, May 28, 1904.

Butterfield, Chapters in Rural Progress, XII.

Butterfield, The Country Church and the Rural Problem, III.

Galloway, "Country Church Problem Analyzed," The Interior, July 23, 1910.

Hayward, Institutional Work for the Country Church, I.

Landis, "The Rural Church," Religious Education, December, 1909.

Raymond, "The Church of Christ in Ruralville," Yale Divinity Quarterly, February, 1909.

Roads, Rural Christendom, XVIII.

Report of the Country Life Commission, 60-63.

QUESTIONS ON CHAPTER III

Aim: To Show the Necessity for Adequate Educational Facilities for Country Life

1. To what extent are we under obligation to the Church for our secular system of education?
2.* Why does the state consider it necessary to provide for the education of its youth?
3. What do you consider some of the outstanding benefits of popular education?
4.* What contributions does the public school make to the Church?
5. Why are promotion of education and the Protestant Church so closely associated?
6. To what extent is agricultural prosperity dependent upon good schools?
7.* Do you believe that the course of study in a rural school should differ from that in a city school? Give reasons.
8. Will it ever be possible to eliminate all one-room schools in our rural communities? Give reasons.
9.* What are some of the advantages of a centralized school?

10. Under what conditions is it possible to establish centralized schools?
11. What are some of the requirements, aside from a well-equipped building, for a first-class school?
12. Name some of the distinct contributions that the extension work of agricultural colleges can make.
13. Do you believe that the Church should promote agricultural education among the people? State reasons for or against.
14.* What is the aim of the Sunday-school?
15. Do you believe that the Sunday-school has fulfilled its mission when it has imparted instruction regarding the Bible?
16. Should the Sunday-school include in its curriculum courses on missions, social service, patriotism, and good citizenship?
17. In what ways can the weekly Sunday-school teachers' meeting render service to the local community?
18. Are the public schools sufficient to meet all the needs of a country community?
19. Is the extension work of the State agricultural colleges sufficient to meet all the needs of the country community?
20. Sum up in the order of their importance the principal educational needs in our rural communities.
21.* What can the Church do to meet these needs?

REFERENCES FOR ADVANCED STUDY

CHAPTER III

Anderson, The Country Town, 24, 217, 252-255.
Ashenhurst, The Day of the Country Church, IX.
Bailey, The Country Life Movement, 61-84.
Butterfield, The Country Church and the Rural Problem, 46-55.
Butterfield, Chapters in Rural Progress, IX, XVI.
Carver, Principles of Rural Economics, 359-361.
Foght, The American Rural School, passim.
Miller, The Problems of the Town Church, XX.
Plunkett, The Rural Life Problem of the United States, 132-135.
Report of the Country Life Commission, 53-56.
Roads, Rural Christendom, XIV.
Vincent, The Modern Sunday School, XVII.

QUESTIONS ON CHAPTER IV

AIM: TO LEARN HOW THE MORAL LIFE OF THE RURAL COM-
MUNITY MAY BE IMPROVED

1. Is it natural for people to desire some form of recreation and amusement?

2.* Are amusements a factor in the development of the morals of the people?

3. Can you give concrete incidents in which amusements have affected the morals of people?

4. Would you consider the barroom a place of amusement?

5. If places of amusement are closed by law, are the citizens responsible for good substitutes?

6. To what extent shall the church of a community provide wholesome amusements and recreation?

7. Make a list of the wholesome amusements a church can consistently offer to a community?

8. What are some of the general principles you would adopt in furnishing amusement and recreation through the Church?

9. Would you offer these amusements only to young people connected with your church?

10. Under what supervision would you offer amusements to the people of your community?

11.* Enumerate some of the moral benefits that can come to young men by participation in baseball, football, and other athletic exercises?

12. What do you consider some of the benefits that accrue to an individual from coöperation in play?

13. State the influences for good and evil that the spirit of speculation has upon individuals?

14.* What Bible texts would you use in preaching to men in the speculative period?

15. What do you consider the greatest need of the man mentioned on page 90, who sent his milk to Buffalo instead of Rochester?

16. How would you reach the man mentioned on page 90, who provided milk from a grass-fed cow to a sick child in the community, but sent his milk from cows fed on green corn to the city?

17.* What recommendations would you make to teach an individual to practise the Golden Rule?

18.* Discuss lines of activity that the Church can promote to improve the moral life of the people.

REFERENCES FOR ADVANCED STUDY

CHAPTER IV

Anderson, The Country Town, XVII.

Ashenhurst, The Day of the Country Church, VI.

Bailey, The Country Life Movement, 97-133.

Butterfield, Chapters in Rural Progress, XIV.

Butterfield, The Country Church and the Rural Problem, 36-44.

Conn, "Federation of Rural Social Forces," Charities, November 3, 1908.

Hayward, Institutional Work for the Country Church, V, IX.

Hyde, "The Social Mission of the Country Church." Minutes of the National Council of the Congregational Churches of the United States, Portland, October, 1901.

Mead, Modern Methods in Church Work, II, IX, XII, XIX, XXI, XXII.

Miller, The Problem of the Town Church, IX, XVI.

Roads, Rural Christendom, XV-XVII.

Wilson, Quaker Hill, Part I, chs. V, VII.

QUESTIONS ON CHAPTER V

AIM: TO REALIZE THE BENEFITS THAT WOULD COME FROM ECONOMIC COÖPERATION AND CHURCH FEDERATION

1. What conditions among pioneer farmers made coöperation impossible?

2. Why does not the household farmer coöperate easily with others?

3. What effect has the speculative spirit upon economic coöperation?

4. Name some of the foremost examples of community coöperation in the United States.

5. What is the difference between coöperative farming and a labor union?

6. What is the difference between coöperative farming and communism?

7.* Name some of the concessions that must be made by individuals who coöperate.

8. What are some of the direct benefits that accrue to a community through economic coöperation?

9. Enumerate some of the activities that can be done more effectively by coöperation.

10. What are the strength and weakness of the Grange as at present organized?

11. What lessons can we learn from the results of coöperation in Denmark?

12. What religious message would you deliver to a community that refused to coöperate?

13. To what extent is Church federation dependent upon economic coöperation?

14. Name some conditions under which you would recommend the federation of Churches.

15. Do you believe that one strong church can do more for a community than several weak ones?

16. Would you recommend federation in a community that is increasing in population if the churches were fairly prosperous?

17.* Name some of the sacrifices that four leading Protestant communions would be obliged to make if they federated into one body.

18.* Name the points of belief in which there is harmony of belief in these communions.

19.* Sum up the losses and gains that would result in such a federation.

20. Quote passages of Scripture that seem to express the spirit of unity and federation.

REFERENCES FOR ADVANCED STUDY

CHAPTER V

Coöperation.

Bailey, The Country Life Movement, 149-164.

Butterfield, Chapters in Rural Progress, XVII.

Carver, Principles of Rural Economics, 274, 278.

Carver, "Rural Economy as a Factor in the Success of the Church." Department of Social and Public Service, Bulletin No. 4.

Plunkett, The Rural Life Problem of the United States, V.

Federation.

Ashenhurst, The Day of the Country Church, X, XI.

Butterfield, The Country Church and the Rural Problem, 64-72, 114-116.

Hooker, "The Problem of Interdenominational Comity Among Country Churches in Home Missionary Territory; Christianity Practically Applied. Report of Chicago Conference of the Evangelical Alliance, 1893.

Root, "Overcoming Our Overlapping," The Home Missionary, November, 1908.
Strong, The New Era, XIV.
Wells, "How Two Country Churches Became One," The Watchman, March 17, 1910.

QUESTIONS ON CHAPTER VI

AIM: To Realize the Necessity for the Abolition of Poverty and the Generous Support of the Church

1. What is the difference between a pauper and a poor man as defined by the author?
2. How do you account for the increase in the number of tenant farmers in productive sections?
3. How do you account for a larger proportion of poor in the most prosperous States?
4. How do you interpret the words of Jesus: "Blessed are ye poor, for yours is the kingdom of God"?
5. Are the poor more religious as a rule than those who are wealthy? Give reasons.
6.* What selfish motives can you suggest for taking care of the poor in your community?
7. Quote passages of Scripture that command the care of the poor.
8. Do you believe that the Church, coöperating with the people and other agencies, can abolish poverty in a rural community?
9. Name some of the principles suggested by the author for successful church finances.
10. Do you believe in asking poor people to contribute toward the work of the church? Why?
11.* Do you believe that it is more blessed to give than to receive?
12. Name some of the advantages of the duplex envelope system.
13. Should the personal canvass for financial support be conducted by the minister or officers of the church?
14.* What obligations has a church outside of its own community?
15. Quote passages of Scripture that illustrate the principle and practise of giving.
16. How much salary do you think a minister should be paid in the country?
17. With what class of people in a community should the minister's salary compare?

18. Is the author's estimate of a minister's salary fair?
19. Do you believe the ordinary rural community can meet these demands?

REFERENCES FOR ADVANCED STUDY

CHAPTER VI

Poverty.

Beard, The Story of John Frederic Oberlin, II, V.
Carver, Principles of Rural Economics, V.
Gladden, Social Salvation, II.
Peabody, Jesus Christ and the Social Question, V.
Rauschenbusch, Christianity and the Social Crisis, 304, 305.

Church Support.

Ashenhurst, The Day of the Country Church, XV.
Butterfield, The Country Church and the Rural Problem, 123-129.
McGarrah, " Raising Money in the Country Church," The Herald and Presbyter, May 4, 1910.
Mead, Modern Methods in Church Work, XXXIX.
Miller, The Problem of the Town Church, XVIII.
Rauschenbusch, Christianity and the Social Crisis, 291-298.
Roads, Rural Christendom, XXII.

QUESTIONS ON CHAPTER VII

AIM: To Learn How the Church May Render Social Service to the People of the Community

1. Define social service.
2. What do you understand by the marginal people of a community?
3.* To what class of people did Jesus minister chiefly?
4. Did Jesus confine his ministry to the souls of men?
5. What is the difference between serving individuals and serving communities?
6.* Is it more important to minister to the poor or to abolish the conditions that cause poverty?
7. Shall the Church direct its ministry to the poor, and neglect the rich?
8. Do you believe the Wisconsin minister rendered

Christian service when he led the people in organizing a coöperative store?

9. Would he have been able to continue his church work if he had not aided them to prosper financially?

10. Name some of the advantages for social service that a minister has who has knowledge of scientific farming.

11. Would you advise theological students who enter country parishes to take agricultural courses?

12.* Enumerate forms of social service for a community in which a minister should lead.

13. What lessons may we learn from the achievements of Mr. Hares, the Minnesota minister, Mr. Adams, and Dr. Persons?

14.* What do you consider some of the vital principles in a campaign for social service in a community?

15. Who are the marginal people in your community?

16. What is being done for them?

17.* Do you believe the Church should engage in social service for the community?

18. Quote passages of Scripture that would warrant the Church in engaging in social service.

REFERENCES FOR ADVANCED STUDY

CHAPTER VII

Social Teachings of Jesus.
Brown, The Social Message of the Modern Pulpit, II.
Gladden, Social Salvation, I.
Peabody, Jesus Christ and the Social Question, II.
Rauschenbusch, Christianity and the Social Crisis, II.
Strong, The Challenge of the City, VI.
Strong, The Next Great Awakening, VI.
Social Service.
Anderson, The Country Town, XVII.
Ashenhurst, The Day of the Country Church, V.
Beard, The Story of John Frederic Oberlin, V.
Hayward, Institutional Work for Country Churches, III, V, VIII, IX, XI.
Mead, Modern Methods in Church Work, XIX, XXI, XXII, XXVI, XXX.
Miller, The Problems of the Town Church, IX, XVI.
Roads, Rural Christendom, VIII-XVII.
Strong, The New Era, XII.
Taylor, "The Civic Function of the Country Church," The Chautauquan, December, 1902.

QUESTIONS ON CHAPTER VIII

AIM: To Realize the Importance of Leadership in a Rural Community

1. Trace the four phases of farming described by the author.
2. Name some of the changes that have taken place in rural communities.
3. Do you believe that farming in the organized period is on a more substantial basis than in any previous era?
4. How do you account for the lack of leadership among rural people?
5. Why do leaders as a rule arise in towns and cities?
6. What type of leaders will reunions and anniversaries develop in a rural community?
7. What type of leaders will religious festivals develop?
8. How can leaders be developed through revival services?
9.* Is the Church as a symbol broader in its service than the Grange, lodge, or political party? Explain fully.
10. Shall the Church in its leadership recognize class distinctions?
11. Did the New England minister make a serious mistake in conducting funerals by not taking account of local sentiments? Give reasons.
12.* What are some of the qualifications for a minister to be successful in a rural community?
13.* In selecting a minister, would you prefer a good preacher or a good organizer? Why?
14. Which type of minister will develop the most local leadership?
15. To what extent is the church-member responsible for the success or failure of a church?
16.* What do you consider the functions of the Church?
17.* Just how may we make the Church of our community the dominating symbol? Discuss fully.
18. Will coöperation and federation aid the Church in holding a more commanding position before the community?
19.* What recommendations can you make to develop and strengthen leadership among country people?

REFERENCES FOR ADVANCED STUDY

CHAPTER VIII

Leadership.

    Anderson, The Country Town, XVI.

    Ashenhurst, The Day of the Country Church, XVIII.

    Beard, The Story of John Frederic Oberlin, passim.

    Butterfield, Chapters in Rural Progress, XII.

    Butterfield, The Country Church and the Rural Problem, V.

    Hayward, Institutional Work for the Country Church, II.

    Hoyt, "The Call of the Country Church." Edited by John R. Mott, 124 East Twenty-eighth Street, New York, 1909.

    McNutt, "Modern Methods in the Country Church."

    Report of the Country Life Commission, 60-65.

    Roads, Rural Christendom, XVIII-XXIII.

    Strong, The New Era, XIII.

APPENDIXES

APPENDIX A

HOW DENMARK DID IT

After several years' war with England in Napoleon Bonaparte's time, Denmark was financially bankrupt, and with a gloomy prospect of another war,—this time at the southern border-line, with Schleswig-Holstein and Germany.

Bishop Grundtvig brooded over his countrymen's dulness and stupidity. He wrote and preached to awaken and stir up the people to patriotism and to revive the spiritual life of the masses. With prophetic sense, he saw that, if salvation is to come, it must come from within, through the enlightenment of all the people, and that the individual must be educated to be more virtuous, more intelligent, more skilful, and more industrious, and to have a true, honest impulse toward self-reform.

His eloquent appeal aroused considerable enthusiasm; his hearers opened their eyes; certain thinkers and statesmen reflected for themselves; others smiled, scorned, and said, "Optimism!"

The movement, however, gained foothold, and the first small Folk High School was started by private individuals, near the southern border-line, in 1844. There were only about twenty pupils during a term for several years. The Queen became interested in Grundtvig's philosophy, and there was talk about founding a popular State High School. But the King, Christian the Eighth, who had promised aid, died, in 1848, and this plan was dropped for the time being.

Probably this was the best for the Folk High Schools as they now are. Instead of one large state school, private schools were established, and in the year 1852 the second Folk High School was opened, out in the country, by a great pedagogical genius, C. Kold. It proved a success, and a few other schools were started during the next ten to twelve years. Kold's method and personality had a great influence upon the movement in the future.

Folk High Schools and Agricultural Schools were established, and have increased from year to year, until at present there are from seventy to eighty Folk High Schools and twenty to twenty-five Agricultural Schools scattered throughout Denmark. All of these schools are owned by private individuals, but receive aid from the government, in proportion to their size. Prospective pupils may also readily receive financial aid from the national and county governments.

By years of experience, it has been found more practical to have the High Schools independent of the Agricultural Schools, but the leading spirit is the same, and the most proficient agricultural student has generally spent one term at the High School.

All these schools are boarding-schools. The professors and teachers, with their families and students, associate together like one large family, and even at the largest ones, with two hundred or more pupils, they have at least dinner together.

Grundtvig lived to see his idea carried into execution. He attended to his voluminous writing and Church work to the last, preaching his last sermon in Vartow Church at Copenhagen a few days before he died (1872), at the age of eighty-nine years.

The population of Denmark is some three million, and about two fifths of the inhabitants are land-tillers. Roughly estimated, about 24,000 young men and women are annually introduced to the world, so to speak. Of these, about 8,000 go to the Folk High Schools every year, for at least one term, which is generally five months in the winter for men, and three months in the summer for women. Others go to the university, seminaries, and technical schools, or trade schools.

Naturally, it would seem incredible, to people unfamiliar with this method of teaching, that the students in the Folk High School could acquire such education, in a comparatively short time, as is frequently attributed to these schools. The public schools are of the highest standard, and are equal to the public schools in any other country, so that the youths when entering the Folk High Schools are fairly well educated in the common branches of study.

At least eighteen years of age is generally required for admission to the Folk High Schools (there is no maximum age), as at this age a person usually grasps new ideas easily. They readily enter into the spirit of the school, and give close attention to their work—which is done without any examinations.

The teaching and instruction are usually in the form of lectures on historical, literary, scientific, religious, and other subjects, the purpose of all of which is to awaken individual personality and the power of thinking, and inspire to activity the intellectual and spiritual life, by popularizing learn-

N. F. S. GRUNDTVIG

ing. This broadens the student's view of his surroundings and the world in general.

The course in the agricultural schools consists of lectures and practical demonstrations of all work connected with a farm.

I might also add that music, singing, and gymnastics play an important part in both of these schools. Undoubtedly the majority leave them with their senses awakened, with an enlarged view of life, and with an impulse of true Christianity, although these schools are not what would be called religious schools, as religion is left to the student's free will. Yet, there is an uplifting religious atmosphere about them which is noticeable.

These youths, naturally, become members, and are among the leaders, of the many different coöperative societies which cover practically everything connected with rural Denmark's welfare, even to the smallest detail, including the importation of general supplies and exportation and sale of their products.

They have their own representatives in the congress, who are elected from among themselves, and at present comprise the leading political party.

The present members of the King's Cabinet are more or less directly interested in the Folk High School movement. Prime Minister Berntsen has been a Folk High School teacher, and the Minister of Education, Appel, is a teacher, and president of the largest Folk High School. The other members of the Cabinet, with a few exceptions, are plain farmers, educated at these schools.

The friendships formed during the High School course are not severed after the student's departure. They have founded societies, which are scattered throughout the country, and in many cases have erected their own buildings, with hotel accommodations. One of the largest organizations of this kind is at Copenhagen, and has about six hundred active members.

In these societies, members and friends assemble amid home-like surroundings for social and educational purposes, and they thus retain the helpful influence which they acquired as students at the schools.

They have also built numerous churches throughout the country, to which ministers are sent who have been chosen by the congregation. Up to a few years ago, the people had little to say about the choice of the clergymen, because the established Church, which is Lutheran, is under the direct control of the state, but the present legislature's tendency is to a greater freedom for the Church.

APPENDIX B

BIBLIOGRAPHY

To prepare a complete list of books, periodicals, references, and pamphlet literature on this subject would be almost an endless task, and probably result in some important omissions. It has therefore seemed wise to print a selected list.

General

Anderson, W L. The Country Town. 1906. Baker & Taylor Co., New York. $1.00, net.
   A careful study of rural evolution, treating the changed conditions, character, selection and environment, and social reconstruction. Confined to New England.

Bailey, L. H. American Agriculture Cyclopedia, 4 Vols. 1907. Macmillan Co., New York. $20.00.
   Exhaustive treatment of farms, climates, soils, crops, animals, and the relation of the farmer to the community.

Bailey, L. H. The Country Life Movement in the United States, 1911. Macmillan Co., New York. $1.25, net.
   A discussion of the country-life movement. Omits a treatment of the relation of the Church.

Bailey, L. H. The State and the Farmer. 1908. Macmillan Co., New York. $1.25.
   An excellent book on rural economics and organization.

Butterfield, K. L. Chapters in Rural Progress. 1908. University of Chicago Press, Chicago. $1.00, net.
   An analysis of some of the more significant phases of the rural problem, and a description of some of the agencies at work in solving it. Perhaps the best general book on the subject.

Carver, T. N. Principles of Rural Economics. 1911. Ginn & Co., Boston. $1.30.
   Includes a discussion of general principles, historical sketch, factors in production, management, distribution, and profits. Should be read by every student of rural life.

Plunkett, Sir Horace. The Rural Life Problem in the United
States. 1910. Macmillan Co., New York. $1.25.
   Notes by a keen observer, based upon thirty-six years'
   experience in Ireland and America. He pleads for or-
   ganization for "better farming, better business, and bet-
   ter living."
Pratt, E. A. The Organization of Agriculture. 1904. E. P.
Dutton, New York. $2.00, net.
   An excellent work describing what is being done in
   the principal countries of Europe and America toward
   the better organization of the farming interests.
Report of the Country Life Commission, Senate Document,
No. 705. Government Printing Press, Washington. For
sale by Sturgis and Walton, New York. 75 cents, net.
   The result of a survey by experts under the direction
   of the United States Government.
Taylor, H. C. Agricultural Economics. 1905. Macmillan
Co.. New York. $1.25.
   An excellent manual for the study of the economic
   principles underlying agricultural problems.
Wilson, W. H. Quaker Hill. 1907. W. H. Wilson, 156
Fifth Avenue, New York City. $1.25.
   A sociological survey of Quaker Hill, New York.

The Country Church

Abbott, E. H. Religious Life in America. 1902. Macmillan
Co., New York. $1.00.
   A record of personal observations on religious life,
   based upon a journey through eighteen States.
Ashenhurst, J. O. The Day of the Country Church. 1910.
Funk & Wagnalls, New York. $1.00, net.
   A treatment of the opportunity of the country Church
   based upon experience. A stimulating and helpful
   volume.
Beard, A. F. The Story of John Frederic Oberlin. 1909.
Pilgrim Press, Boston. $1.25.
   The story of the marvelous work of Oberlin of Wal-
   dersbach. Indispensable as an account of achievement
   under most difficult circumstances.
Butterfield, K. L. The Country Church and the Rural Prob-
lem. 1911. University of Chicago Press, Chicago. $1.00.
   A series of lectures delivered at Hartford Theological
   Seminary. Suggestive and constructive in its message.
Hayward, C. E. Institutional Work for the Country Church.

1900. Free Press Association, Burlington, Vt. 50 cents.
Contains many valuable hints for effective work.

Roads, Charles. Rural Christendom. 1909. American Sunday School Union, Philadelphia. 90 cents.
A discussion of the rural problem, the agencies for the spread of Christian principles, and the place of the Church in Christianizing the community.

Education

Burton, Ernest D., and Matthews, Shailer. Principles and Ideals of the Sunday School. 1903. University of Chicago Press, Chicago. $1.00.
One of the best books on pedagogy in the Sunday-school.

Cope, Henry F. The Modern Sunday School in Principle and Practice. 1907. Fleming H. Revell Co., New York. $1.00, net.
A helpful statement of the history, organization, principles, and practice of the modern Sunday-school.

Foght, H. W. The American Rural School. 1910. Macmillan Co., New York. $1.25, net.
A most practical book, covering every phase of rural life, especially written for rural school-teachers, superintendents, and school-board members.

Kern, O. J. Among Country Schools. 1906. Ginn & Co., Boston, Mass. $1.25.
Written by a county superintendent of wide experience. Treats of every important phase of rural-school activity.

Vincent, J. H. The Modern Sunday School. 1900. Eaton & Mains, New York. $1.00.
Chapter XVII deals especially with the rural school.

Report of Committee of Twelve on The Rural School. Proceedings of the National Education Association, 1897.

Report of Committee on Industrial Education in Schools for Rural Communities. Proceedings of the National Educational Association, 1907.
Best discussions of fundamental problems.

Christian Sociology

Brown, C. R. The Social Message of the Modern Pulpit. 1906. Charles Scribner's Sons, New York. $1.25.
A message to ministers, setting forth the broad opportunities for social uplift.

Earp, Edwin L. The Social Engineer. 1911. Eaton & Mains, New York. $1.50, net.

A treatment of the essentials for a successful social worker, and a statement of the activities in which one may engage.

Gladden, Washington. Social Salvation. 1902. Houghton, Mifflin & Co., New York. $1.00.

Lectures delivered before the students of the Divinity School of Yale University. A discussion of some of the social problems, with suggested remedies.

Henderson, C. R. Social Duties from a Christian Point of View. 1909. University of Chicago Press, Chicago. $1.25.

A text-book for the study of social problems. Valuable for classes in Christian Sociology. Has a good chapter on social duties in rural communities.

Jenks, J. W. Social Teachings of Jesus. 1906. Y. M. C. A. Press, New York. 75 cents.

The social aspects of Christ's teachings as related to the problems of modern life, treated in a twelve weeks' course.

Patten, S. N. The New Basis of Civilization. 1907. Macmillan Co., New York. $1.00.

An interpretation of the meaning and significance of recent social changes with which the practical social worker is engaged.

Peabody, Francis G. Jesus Christ and the Social Question. 1910. Macmillan Co., New York. $1.50.

An examination of the teachings of Jesus with regard to problems of social life.

Rauschenbusch, Walter. Christianity and the Social Crisis. 1907. Macmillan Co., New York. $1.50.

An able discussion of the social aims of Jesus and the challenge to the Church to carry out the work. One of the most stimulating books on the social question.

Methods of Church Work

Gladden, Washington. Parish Problems. Century Co., New York. $2.00. (Out of print.)

A helpful discussion of the various problems connected with the activities of the Church, Sunday-school, and the community. Contains a chapter on the needs of country churches.

Hayward, C. E. Institutional Work for the Country Church. 1900. Free Press Association, Burlington, Vt. 50 cents.

A practical handbook for country pastors, describing specific methods that have been found practical.

Mead, G. W. Modern Methods in Church Work. 1903. Dodd, Mead & Co., New York. $1.50.

As the title suggests, a discussion of methods of work.

Miller, George A. The Problems of the Town Church. 1902. Fleming H. Revell Co., New York. 75 cents.

Devoted almost wholly to methods of work.

Periodical Articles and Pamphlets

A Chance for the Country Church. The Presbyterian Advance, September 8, 1910.

Anthony, A. W. The Problem of the New England Country Church. Homiletic Review, July, 1899.

Biglow, W. B. The Country Church in America. Scribner's Magazine, November, 1897.

Boyle, J. E. The Passing of the Country Church. The Outlook, May 28, 1904.

Carver, Prof. T. N. Rural Economy as a Factor in the Success of the Church. Department of Social and Public Service, Bulletin No. 4, 20 pp. American Unitarian Association, 25 Beacon St., Boston.

Conn, G. W. Federation of Rural Social Forces. Charities, November 3, 1908.

Coulter, J. L. Organization Among Farmers of the United States. Yale Review, November, 1909.

Country Life and the Church. The Outlook, April 10, 1909.

Galloway, T. W. Country Church Problem Analyzed. The Interior, July 23, 1910.

Gard, H. The Autobiography of a Country School Teacher. World's Work, May, 1910.

Gilbert, G. H. How One Man Saved a Town. The Outlook, April 18, 1908.

Gill, C. O. The Country Church and Recreation. Auburn Seminary Record, March, 1910.

Goodenough, A. H. How to Reach the Rural Population. The Christian Advocate, December 29, 1904.

Hartt, R. L. A New England Hill Town. The Atlantic Monthly, 1899.

Hartt, R. L. The Regeneration of Rural New England. The Outlook, March 3, 10, 17, 31, 1900.

Hitchcock, E. P. Coöperation in Country Life. Country Life, October, 1909.

Hooker, G. E. The Problem of Interdenominational Comity Among Country Churches in Home Missionary Territory, Christianity Practically Applied. Report of Chicago Conference of the Evangelical Alliance, 1893.

Hoyt, A. H. The Call of the Country Church. Young Men's Christian Association Press, New York.

Hyde, W. D. Impending Paganism in New England. The Forum, June, 1892.

Hyde, W. D. The Social Mission of the Country Church. Minutes of the National Council of the Congregational Churches of the United States, Portland, October, 1901.

Kennedy, A. J. Religious Overlapping. The Independent, April 9, May 7, 1908.

Landis, E. B. A Country Minister at Work. Rural Manhood, Vol. I, No. 9.

Landis, E. B. Rural Church in Its Educational and Social Opportunities. Religious Education, Vol. XV, No. 5.

McGarrah, A. F. Raising Money in the Country Church. The Herald and Presbyter, May 4, 1910.

McNutt, M. B. Modern Methods in the Country Church. Missionary Education Movement, New York.

Moral Problems of the Farm. The Outlook, May 29, 1909.

Nesmith, G. T. The Rural Church. American Journal of Sociology, May, 1903.

Plunkett, Sir Horace. Satisfaction in Farm Life. The Outlook, January 20, 1910.

Proceedings of the Conference on the Problems of the Rural Church in New England. Meeting held in Boston, January 18, 19, 1909. Report of N. E. Country Church Associations. Address H. K. Rowe, Newton Center, Mass.

Taylor, Graham. The Civic Function of the Country Church. The Chautauquan, December, 1902.

The Country Church. The Westminster, February 12, 1910.

The Country Church and Its Social Problem. The Outlook, August 18, 1906.

The Country Church and the Making of Manhood. The Homiletic Review, August, 1907. Pamphlet reprint. 6 pp. 10 cents, postpaid.

The Useless Tragedy of the Farmer's Wife. The Delineator, June, 1909.

Two Country Church Numbers. The Congregationalist and Christian World, July, 1904, 1905.

Wells, G. F. An Answer to the New England Country Church Question. The Bibliotheca Sacra, April, 1907. Pamphlet reprint. 10 pp. 10 cents, postpaid.

Wells, G. F. Church Federation as a Practical Proposition. The Christian Advocate, New York, March 29, April 5, 1906.

Wells, G. F. How Two Country Churches Became One. The Watchman, March 17, 1910.

Wright, G. F. The Country Church. The Bibliotheca Sacra, April, 1890.

INDEX

229

Forward Mission Study Courses

"Anywhere, *provided it be* FORWARD."—*David Livingstone.*

Prepared under the direction of the

MISSIONARY EDUCATION MOVEMENT

OF THE UNITED STATES AND CANADA

EDITORIAL COMMITTEE: T. H. P. Sailer, *Chairman;* A. E. Armstrong, T. B. Ray, H. B. Grose, J. E. McAfee, C. R. Watson, A. R. Gray, L. B. Wolf, G. F. Sutherland, H. P. Douglass.

The Forward Mission Study Courses are an outgrowth of a conference of leaders in young people's mission work, held in New York City, December, 1901. To meet the need that was manifested at that conference for mission study text-books suitable for young people, two of the delegates, Professor Amos R. Wells, of the United Society of Christian Endeavor, and Mr. S. Earl Taylor, Chairman of the General Missionary Committee of the Epworth League, projected the Forward Mission Study Courses. These courses have been officially adopted by the Missionary Education Movement, and are now under the immediate direction of the Editorial Committee of the Movement. The books of the Movement are now being used by more than forty home and foreign mission boards and societies of the United States and Canada.

The aim is to publish a series of text-books covering the various home and foreign mission fields and written by leading authorities.

The following text-books having a sale of 900,000 have been published:

1. THE PRICE OF AFRICA. (Biographical.) By S. Earl Taylor.

2. INTO ALL THE WORLD. A general survey of missions. By Amos R. Wells.

3. PRINCELY MEN IN THE HEAVENLY KINGDOM. (Biographical.) By Harlan P. Beach.

4. SUNRISE IN THE SUNRISE KINGDOM. A study of Japan. By John H. DeForest.

5. HEROES OF THE CROSS IN AMERICA. Home Missions. (Biographical.) By Don O. Shelton.

6. DAYBREAK IN THE DARK CONTINENT. A study of Africa. By Wilson S. Naylor.

7. THE CHRISTIAN CONQUEST OF INDIA. A study of India. By James M. Thoburn.

8. ALIENS OR AMERICANS? A study of Immigration. By Howard B. Grose.

9. THE UPLIFT OF CHINA. A study of China. By Arthur H. Smith.

10. THE CHALLENGE OF THE CITY. A study of the City. By Josiah Strong.

11. THE WHY AND HOW OF FOREIGN MISSIONS. A study of the relation of the home Church to the foreign missionary enterprise. By Arthur J. Brown.

12. THE MOSLEM WORLD. A study of the Mohammedan World. By Samuel M. Zwemer.

13. THE FRONTIER. A study of the New West. By Ward Platt.

14. SOUTH AMERICA: Its Missionary Problems. A study of South America. By Thomas B. Neely.

15. THE UPWARD PATH: The Evolution of a Race. A study of the Negro. By Mary Helm.

16. KOREA IN TRANSITION. A study of Korea. By James S. Gale.

17. ADVANCE IN THE ANTILLES. A study of Cuba and Porto Rico. By Howard B. Grose.

18. THE DECISIVE HOUR OF CHRISTIAN MISSIONS. A study of conditions throughout the non-Christian world. By John R. Mott.

19. INDIA AWAKENING. A study of present conditions in India. By Sherwood Eddy.

20. THE CHURCH OF THE OPEN COUNTRY. A study of the problem of the rural Church. By Warren H. Wilson.

In addition to these courses, the following have been published especially for use among younger persons:

1. UGANDA'S WHITE MAN OF WORK. The story of Alexander Mackay of Africa. By Sophia Lyon Fahs.

2. SERVANTS OF THE KING. A series of eleven sketches of famous home and foreign missionaries. By Robert E. Speer.

3. UNDER MARCHING ORDERS. The story of Mary Porter Gamewell of China. By Ethel Daniels Hubbard.

4. WINNING THE OREGON COUNTRY. The story of Marcus Whitman and Jason Lee in the Oregon Country. By John T. Faris.

These books are published by mutual arrangement among the home and foreign mission boards, to whom all orders should be addressed. They are bound uniformly and are sold at 50 cents, in cloth, and 35 cents, in paper; postage, 8 cents extra.